TEST
YOUR
NUMERICAL
APTITUDE

TEST
YOUR
NUMERICAL
APTITUDE

How to assess your numeracy skills
and plan your career

JIM BARRETT

**KOGAN
PAGE**

London and Philadelphia

First published in Great Britain and the United States in 2007 by Kogan Page Limited

120 Pentonville Road
London N1 9JN
United Kingdom
www.kogan-page.co.uk

525 South 4th Street, #241
Philadelphia PA 19147
USA

© Jim Barrett, 2007

ISBN 978 0 7494 5064 9

British Library Cataloguing-in-Publication Data

A CIP record for this book is available from the British Library.

Library of Congress Cataloging-in-Publication Data

Barrett, James.
    Test your numerical aptitude / Jim Barrett.
        p. cm.
    Includes bibliographical references.
    ISBN-13: 978-0-7494-5064-9
    ISBN-10: 0-7494-5064-9
1. Numeracy--Problems, exercises, etc. 2. Ability--Testing. I. Title.
    QA141.B34 2007
    513.076--dc22

                                                            2007022036

Typeset by Saxon Graphics Ltd, Derby
Printed and bound in Great Britain by Creative Print and Design (Wales), Ebbw Vale

Contents

Introduction

It is surprising how many people, including those who are highly intelligent and well educated, even to degree and professional level, suffer from apprehension about numerical tests. All too often, lack of confidence, not aptitude, is the reason for their failure pass a test or an exam, obtain a job or be selected for a training course.

Because people are unsure of what may be expected of them they may underperform on tests and assessments, even though they have the innate potential to do well and make appropriate career progression. Unfortunately, they may even hold back from applying for a job or course in the first place. What a waste of talent!

At the same time, the requirement to work with some form of numbers at work is growing. And there are always more opportunities for people who are willing to use their numerical aptitude.

It is strange that as demand for numerical aptitude from employers is increasing, the supply, or aptitude, does not appear to keep up with it. For this reason, many employers, as well as universities, do not trust exam results and may prefer to search out the talent themselves. Thus, more organizations are setting their own tests of key aptitudes, numbers being one of the high priority areas. Yet, numbers have not changed: although numbers may be used in different ways as new patterns of work are created, the basic ways of using numbers have always been the same.

This book intends to reassure you of the ways numbers are used and applied, and suggest how you can succeed with your underlying aptitude for numbers. When you know what you are capable of and what to expect, there is little need for fear; it makes sense to provide yourself with the means to take advantage of the opportunities that are available to you.

I know of professional people who have worked through the numerical tests in my earlier books as preparation before an assessment for a new job or because a new role demanded greater familiarity and use of numbers. This book is distinct because it is designed to concentrate many different types of numerical tests in a single volume. It intends to provide comprehensive coverage of what can be expected in many real life working, exam and test situations. Additionally, there are exercises that investigate your personality and motivation, thus enabling you to think how your particular type of numerical aptitude might suit different careers.

This book looks at numerical aptitude, that is, the underlying talent a person possesses in order to understand and use numbers. It does not look at acquired skills, for example the level of ability that is the product of educational courses at school or college in mathematics, business studies, economics, accounts or computer science. However, if a person has the underlying ability, it may help to point them in one of these directions or even 'brush them up' in areas in which they feel they may be lacking.

This book makes every attempt to be 'fair' by trying to establish a 'level playing field' for everybody who takes each test. This is important because it is true that familiarity in working with numbers will allow someone to develop specific numerical skills. But, to be 'fair' everyone should have an equal chance at the start. Therefore, Part 1 is a preparation containing plenty of examples and explanation in order that there will be no unexpected or surprising problem that confronts you. Parts 1 and 2 present you with a range of tests that are similar to those commonly used by organizations for aptitude testing. This book hopes to reassure you that there will be no test about which you say, 'I just couldn't do it; it was too difficult', or, 'It caught me out', so that you may in the future be confident about numerical aptitude tests.

Timed and power tests

Of course, most of the tests are deliberately designed to get harder as you proceed, but all the skills required to solve the problems are provided before you start. There may well be a limit to what you can do in the time allowed by each test. It is essential to know what your 'timed limit' is because this gives an indication of level by which there can be some basis of comparison with everybody else. Your limit may also have another purpose in suggesting where you may need to work harder in your course of study, before an assessment or in your work.

Naturally, people work at different rates and in different ways on the same task. Therefore, a timed test may not fully reveal a person's top limit of aptitude since they may not have had sufficient time to get to the harder problems and thus demonstrate the full range of their proficiency. Speed is not necessarily everything: some people spend more time checking through their answer than others; some people are relating the problem they are working on to other problems or possibilities, an imaginative process not always measured by the test. Yet aspects such as these may be important in the 'real world of work' in which their numerical aptitudes are applied, if not in the test situation itself.

Therefore, the 'power' test looks at what a person is capable of doing where the timed element is taken out. This ensures that you encounter the full range of problems at all levels of difficulty in the type of aptitude being tested. The basis of comparison is with what you are capable of doing as opposed to how quickly you are capable of doing it. Achieving above average marks on either 'time' or 'power' indicates possible career opportunity.

When taking each test it is possible to take it as a timed or power test, or both, by noting your progress after the timed period, then going on to complete the entire test.

Making sense of the aptitude tests

There are two questions: 1) What does my score mean? and 2) What can my score guide me towards?

Firstly, at the end of each test your score or scores can be compared with an assumed average. This compares you with everyone else or 'the general population', as it is known statistically. This allows you some insight as to whether you have a talent greater than that of most other people. Admittedly, the average is no more than a guideline, since it does not reflect any real statistical or measured average in relation to a specific group. But the more you are above average, the more likely it is that you have an aptitude that has a special value because it is comparatively rare and therefore provides you with more career opportunity than most.

Then, your scores on each test can be compared to indicate where your strengths probably lie. These scores can also be related to an intelligence quotient (IQ) scale, which is a quick way to compare your aptitude with a level at which people achieve awards, such as degrees or professional qualifications, or work in senior jobs in which it is essential to possess some form of numerical aptitude.

With regard to the answer to the second question, there are also some suggestions as to the type of work that proficiency on the test might lead to. These are not intended to be specific or exclusive simply because, in the real world, activities can assume a different character due to the manner of working or the nature of the work undertaken in an organization. It is not always realized that numbers are not merely signs, but they can also have meaning and value, depending on how they are regarded and treated. For example, the value placed on numerical accuracy may vary widely. Similarly, where a career is suggested as maybe having a connection with an aptitude, this will also depend on the nature of the organization and the specific situation. The same aptitude may well have a stronger connection with what appears to be a very different type of career due to the circumstances in which the career exists.

Scheme for career guidance

Your numerical talent does not exist separately from the wider repertoire that embraces what you like to do and the way you like to express yourself. All these other aspects will in different ways have an effect on shaping and directing your career. In fact, it might well be asserted that your aptitude is the combination of all of your separate talents, whether they are intellectual or determined by your personality and inclinations. However, the following scheme produces a system that can sort your aptitudes in accordance with different careers that may relate to them.

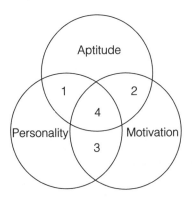

Whereas overlap arises in areas 1, 2 and 3, it is in area 4 that all three elements combine and this is the ideal place to pursue your career simply because this area possesses the greatest congruence of all you are capable of doing and want to do. Having completed all the tests in the book, your task is to see which careers from the Careers list (see page 169) combine all the elements of your aptitudes, personality and motivation.

Number tutor

In Part 1 you will revise and practise basic numerical methods to ensure that you are prepared for the 'real thing'.

This book is not a mathematics text book. Therefore, there is no instruction on mathematical formulae where acquired knowledge is examined by attainment, ability or skills tests.

In this book:

+ means add or plus
− means subtract or take away
* or × means multiply or times
/ or ÷ means divide.

This section provides an explanation of the rules when undertaking basic calculations with numbers. Understanding these rules assures sufficient competence to take aptitude tests from elementary to advanced levels.

All numerical tests involve adding, taking away, dividing or multiplying numbers. Even the most abstract tests use these basic, simple ways of working with numbers. At the outset it is sensible to make yourself as familiar with these principles as you possibly can.

Some parts of this section may be relevant to you, while others will not. Do not proceed to the tests until you have firstly revised the fundamental rules or you already feel confident about what you are to be tested on. Of course, it may well be that the test itself will reveal areas that you need to revise.

In a few cases in this section, you are asked to fill in the figures in calculations. Do not mark the book if it is not your own, write your answers on a separate sheet instead.

Number usage

How to add (or sum)

1. What is 35 and 42?

Putting the numbers under each other in columns makes summing easier.
The column on the right is the units column.
The left column next to the units column is the tens column.
Draw a line under the numbers to be added and draw another line under the space where the answer will be. This gives you an 'answer box'.
Adding 5 and 2 makes 7 in the units column.
Adding 3 and 4 in the tens column makes 7.

$$\begin{array}{r} 35 \\ +42 \\ \hline 77 \end{array}$$

Answer: 77

2. Add 48 to 27

8 and 7 make 15, which is the same as saying 5 units and 1 ten.
Write the 5 down in the units column, but carry the 1 over into the tens column, slightly beneath your answer box. This is essential to remind you to add it together with the other numbers in the tens column.
Now add 1, 2 and 4, which makes 7.

$$\begin{array}{r} 48 \\ +27 \\ \hline 75 \\ \scriptstyle 1 \end{array}$$

Answer: 75

3. What is the sum of 233, 16, 7 and 499?

The first step is to place the numbers in columns of units, tens and hundreds.
Adding the units, 9 + 7 + 6 + 3 comes to 25. The 5 is written in the units column and the 2 is carried over and written into the tens column.
Adding all the tens, 2 + 9 + 1 + 3 comes to 15. The 5 is written in the tens column and the 1 in the hundreds column.
Adding the hundreds, 1 + 4 + 2 comes to 7.

$$
\begin{array}{r}
233 \\
+\ 16 \\
+\ \ 7 \\
+499 \\
\hline
755 \\
\hline
\scriptstyle 12
\end{array}
$$

Answer: 755

4. Find the sum of 4617, 297, 85, 2008 and 450.

Add this up for yourself. The 'carry over' numbers have been written in for you already.
With four-figure numbers there are columns for units, tens, hundreds and thousands. Five-figure numbers would have tens of thousands, and so on.
The answer is 7457.

$$
\begin{array}{r}
4617 \\
+\ 297 \\
+\ \ 85 \\
+2008 \\
+\ 450 \\
\hline
\scriptstyle 122
\end{array}
$$

How to subtract (or take away)

1. Take 53 from 96
Place the numbers in columns of units and tens.
Taking 3 from 6 leaves 3.
Taking 5 from 9 leaves 4.

$$
\begin{array}{r}
96 \\
-53 \\
\hline
43
\end{array}
$$

Answer: 43

2. What is the difference between 726 and 821?
Place the higher number above the lower number.
It is not possible to take away 6 from 1, so a ten is used or borrowed from the tens column. Taking 6 from 11 leaves 5, which is written in your answer box. Thus, 821 has become 811. It is a good idea to put a line through the 2 and to write in the number 1 above it to remind you. Now you have to take 2 away from 1. As this is not possible either it is necessary this time to borrow a hundred. The 8 therefore becomes 7. You can cross through the 8 and write in 7.
Taking 7 from 7 leaves nothing.

```
  71
 821
-726
  95
```

Answer: 95

3. Take 343 from 1010
Fill the figures in for yourself.
You cannot take 3 away from 0, so you borrow a ten, which makes the 1 in the top figure in the tens column a 0. This has been put in to remind you.
Then it is not possible to take 4 from a 0, so you borrow a hundred, which makes the 0 a 9.
Now you can take 3 from the 9.
The answer is 667.

```
   90
 1010
 -343
 ----
```

How to multiply (or times)

1. What is 364 times 3?
3 times 4 is 12. Write the 2 in the units column and carry over the 1, making a note of it in the tens column.
3 times 6 is 18 and adding the 1 carried over makes 19. Write the 9 in the tens column and carry over the 1, making a note of the 1 in the hundreds column.
3 times 3 is 9 and adding the 1 makes 10. The 0 goes in the hundreds column and the 1 goes in the thousands column.

$$\begin{array}{r} 364 \\ \times\,3 \\ \hline 1092 \\ \scriptstyle 11 \end{array}$$

Answer: 1092

2. Multiply 426 by 35
Multiply in order by the units, then the tens. So, 6 by 5 is 30. Place the 0 in the units column and carry over the 3, writing it under the tens column to be added in a moment.
2 by 5 gives 10 and adding 3 gives 13. Place the 3 in the tens column and the 1 in the hundreds column to be added later.
4 by 5 is 20, plus 1 is 21.
As you are now going to multiply by a figure in the tens column, first of all place a 0 in the units column. You can then multiply 6 by 3, which gives 18. Write the 8 in the tens column and the 1 in the hundreds column.
2 by 3 gives 6 and add 1, which gives 7 to be written in the hundreds column. There is nothing to carry over this time.
4 by 3 gives 12.
Now add 2130 to 12780 in the usual way.

$$\begin{array}{r} 426 \\ \times\,35 \\ \hline 2130 \\ \scriptstyle 13 \\ \hline 12780 \\ \scriptstyle 1 \\ \hline 14910 \end{array}$$

Answer: 14910

3. A travel company has 24 planes all of which carry an average of 156 passengers each day. How many people travel each day?

Fill the figures in for yourself.

Multiply by the units 4 figure first, then by the tens figure 2.

The 'carry over' figures have been written in to guide you.

Do not forget to place a 0 in the units' column when you multiply by the 2, which makes sure you keep your figures in the correct columns.

The answer: is 3744.

$$
\begin{array}{r}
156 \\
\times\ 24 \\
\hline
22 \\
11 \\
\hline
\end{array}
$$

How to divide

1. How many fives are there in 360?

The usual method is to write the problem as $5\overline{)360}$, that is, 5 into 360.

Divide 5 into each number in turn.

5 does not go into 3, but 5 goes into 36 7 times. Write the 7 above the 6. Write 35 under the 36.

Take 35 away from 36, which leaves a remainder of 1. Bring down the 0 that has not yet been divided into. Placed by the remainder of 1 it makes 10.

5 into 10 gives 2. Place the 2 above the 0 in the original figure. There is no further remainder.

You can see how important it is to keep all the columns correctly underneath each other.

$$
\begin{array}{r}
72 \\
5\overline{)360} \\
35\ (5 \times 7) \\
10\ (5 \times 2)
\end{array}
$$

Answer: 72

2. What is 2985 divided by 14?
It is essential to get the numbers exactly underneath each other in the correct columns.
14 goes into 29 twice with 1 left over.
Bring down the 8. 14 goes into 18 once with 4 left over.
Bring down the 5.
14 into 45 goes three times with 3 left over or remaining.

$$
\begin{array}{r}
213 \\
14\overline{)2985} \\
28 \ (14 \times 2) \\
\hline
1 \\
18 \\
14 \ (14 \times 1) \\
\hline
4 \\
45 \\
42 \ (14 \times 3) \\
\hline
3 \\
\end{array}
$$

Answer: 213, remainder 3

3. How many eggs will be left over if there are 3455 eggs and 12 eggs can be fitted into each box?
You can fill in the figures for yourself. The answer is 11.

$$
\begin{array}{r}
12\overline{)3455} \\
(12 \times 2) \\
\hline
\\
(12 \times 8) \\
\hline
\\
(12 \times 7) \\
\hline
\end{array}
$$

How to use numbers that are less than zero

1. What is 7 + 3 − 4 − 5 − 3 − 1 = ?
Add all the positive numbers and subtract all the negative numbers.

$$
\begin{array}{r}
7 + 3 = \ \ 10 \\
-4 - 5 - 3 - 1 = -13 \\
\hline
3 \\
\end{array}
$$

Answer: −3

2. What is + 59 and − 278?
Always place the larger number over the smaller. The positive small number is taken away in the same way as if it were negative. Remember to put the minus sign in front of the answer because there were more negatives than positives.

$$
\begin{array}{r}
-278 \\
59 \\
\hline
-219 \\
\end{array}
$$

Answer: −219

3. Add −243 +19 + 99 − 31 − 12 + 76 Add all the negatives. Add all the positives. Take the smaller number from the larger. If the larger number is negative the answer will be negative.	$\begin{array}{rr} -243 & +19 \\ -31 & +99 \\ \underline{-12} & \underline{+76} \\ -286 & +194 \\ & -286 \\ & \underline{+194} \\ & \overline{-92} \end{array}$
	Answer: −92

How to work with series of numbers (sequences)

1. What number comes next? 12 10 8 6 ? The numbers reduce from left to right. 2 is taken away each time.	Answer: 4
2. What number comes next? 2 5 11 23 47 95 ? The numbers increase from left to right. Each number is double the previous number plus 1.	Answer: 191
3. What is the missing number? 2 3 4 6 6 9 8 ? 10 15 12 There are two sequences, which have been put together. 2, 4, 6, 8, 10, 12 and 3, 6, 9, 12, 15.	Answer: 12

How to work with averages and ratios

1. What is the average of 4, 7, 8 and 9? To find the average add all the quantities and divide by the number of the quantities. There are four numbers. The total is divided by the number of quantities.	$4 + 7 + 8 + 9 = 28$ $28 \div 4$ Answer: 7
2. What is the average time to complete a journey if recorded times were 1 hour 50 minutes, 2 hours 10 minutes, 2 hours 40 minutes, 2 hours 15 minutes and 1 hour 5 minutes?	Total hours = 10 Journeys = 5 Answer: 2 hours
3. If there are 8 boys in a class and 12 girls, what is the ratio of boys to girls? A ratio compares one quantity with another. It is common to reduce (simplify) ratios to the smallest possible whole numbers.	8 to 12 or 8 : 12 or 2 : 3 Answer: 2 : 3
4. What is the ratio of the following articles to each other: 15 books, 25 newspapers and 10 magazines?	15 : 25 : 10 or 3 : 5 : 2 Answer: 3 : 5 : 2
5. What proportion of the number of articles are newspapers? Proportion is another word for ratio. It is a part of the whole or total number. In this case, the total is $3 + 5 + 2 = 10$. Newspapers are 5 parts out of 10.	Answer: 1 : 2 (or ½)

Applying numbers

Using numbers to solve real problems requires understanding of some basic principles. Strictly speaking, real-life, or practical, tests measure ability rather than underlying aptitude, but because the type of calculation required is thought to be so familiar to most people, they are often used as indicators of aptitude. At the outset it is sensible to make yourself as familiar with the principles as you possibly can.

How to work with decimals

1. What is meant by the decimal fraction 2567.906?
Whole numbers are to the left of the decimal point and parts of a number to the right.
The first number to the left indicates units (7 in the number above) then tens of units, hundreds, thousands, ten of thousands, and so on. The first number to the right of the decimal point indicates tenths parts of a unit (9 parts of one unit in the number above) then hundredths parts, 0 in this case, and so on.

Answer: Two thousand units, five hundred units, six tens units, seven units, nine tenths units, zero hundredths units and 6 thousandths units.

2. Add 3.456, 65.09, 303 and 42.007
Always place the decimal point of each number exactly under the others. Add like any other sum. Zero has been added to some of the numbers to ensure that the columns are kept in order so as to reduce the chance of error when counting.

$$\begin{array}{r} 3.456 \\ +65.090 \\ +303.000 \\ +42.007 \\ \hline 413.553 \\ {\scriptstyle 11 \quad 11} \end{array}$$

Answer: 413.553

3. What needs to be added to the decimal fraction 2567.906 to turn it into a whole number?

To make (or convert) a decimal fraction to a whole number it is necessary to add enough to the parts of a unit on the right of the decimal point in order to make a unit, which is then shown on the left of the decimal point. Simply place the decimal fraction under the next whole number and take it away in order to show what must be added.

Remember to keep the decimal points underneath each other for ease of working. Also, it is helpful to add zeros to the whole number to aid the subtraction process.

In this case, the process is: 6 cannot be taken from 0, borrow one to make 10, 6 from 10 leaves 4, 0 from 9 leaves 9, and 9 from 9 leaves 0. The 8 in the whole number has now become a 7, having been reduced to the same size as the decimal fraction.

$$
\begin{array}{r}
7\ 9\ 9 \\
2568.000 \\
-2567.906 \\
\hline
.094
\end{array}
$$

Answer: .094

4. Multiply 4.7 by 5.04

Just multiply the two numbers as if the decimal point did not exist. 4 by 7 is 28, so the 2 is carried over into the next column. 4 by 4 is 16 plus 2 is 18. So, 47 by 4 is 188. Next, 47 by 0 is nothing, so there is nothing to write down. Finally, write in two zeros because you are multiplying by a 5, which is in the hundreds column. Then, 5 by 7 is 35, so the 3 is carried over into the next column. 5 by 4 is 20, plus 3 is 23. 188 plus 23500 is 23688.

$$
\begin{array}{r}
4.7 \\
\times\ 5.04 \\
\hline
188 \\
2 \\
23500 \\
3 \\
\hline
23688
\end{array}
$$

After multiplying, count the number of figures, including zeros, there are on the right side of the decimal point. In the sum there are three figures: 7, 0 and 4, so three figures. Count back three figures from the right of your answer to find the correct place for the decimal point.

Answer: 23.688

5. What is 0.307 by 4.007?
Set out the figures in the usual way with the decimal points under each other. Multiply, ignoring the decimal points. There are six figures in total to the right of the decimal points, so there must also be six figures to the right in your answer. Do the calculations yourself although the answer has been given.

$$\begin{array}{r} 0.307 \\ \times\ 4.007 \\ \hline 1.230149 \end{array}$$

Answer: 1.230149

6. Divide 37.06 by 0.4
When dividing decimals, the number you are dividing by (the divisor) needs to be turned into a whole number. In this case, with 0.4, the decimal point needs to be moved one space to the right to become 4. As the decimal point has been moved one space to the right in one number, the same thing needs to be done to the number that is being divided into, making the number 370.6
Divide as usual, but ensure that the decimal points are kept in line with each other. Note that a zero has been brought down so that 4 can be divided into 20 to finish the sum.

$$\begin{array}{r} 92.65 \\ 4\overline{)370.60} \\ 36 \\ \hline 10 \\ 8 \\ \hline 26 \\ 24 \\ \hline 20 \end{array}$$

Answer: 37.06 can be divided by 0.4, 92.65 times.

7. What is 0.018/0.09?
In this case the decimal point must be
moved two places to the right of the
divisor to make the whole number 9.
Doing the same thing to the number to be
divided into makes 1.8.

Answer: 0.2

How to work with fractions

1. Which is the largest fraction: $\dfrac{2}{3}, \dfrac{3}{4}, \dfrac{5}{6}$?

The question asks whether 2 parts of a
whole unit cut into 3, or 3 parts of a unit
cut into 4 or 5 parts of a unit cut into 6
is the largest.

Firstly, make sure all the units look the
same by making the number under the line
(the denominator) the same. This is done
by finding the smallest number that all
the numbers beneath the line of every
fraction will divide into. In this case, the
number is 12.

Then, increase each number above the line
by the same proportion. Thus, there are
four 3s in 12, three 4s in 12 and two 6s
in 12. Therefore, multiply the number of
times each one goes into 12 by the number
above the line. It can be seen that 10 out
of 12 parts is the largest.

$\dfrac{2}{3}, \dfrac{3}{4}, \dfrac{5}{6}$

becomes

$\dfrac{8}{12}, \dfrac{9}{12}, \dfrac{10}{12}$

Answer: $\dfrac{5}{6}$

2. Add $\frac{2}{3}$, $\frac{3}{5}$, and $\frac{1}{10}$

It is important to make sure the denominators are all the same to add all the parts equally. In this case, the lowest denominator that all the fractions can divide into is 30.

The top figures are multiplied by 10 (30/3), 6 (30/5) and 3 (30/10).

The top figures are added. 41 is a 'top heavy' figure. It is usual to resolve this by dividing the bottom figure into the top one. The result is one whole part and 11 parts of 30 left over.

$$\frac{2}{3}, \frac{3}{5}, \text{ and } \frac{1}{10}$$

becomes

$$\frac{20}{30}, \frac{18}{30}, \text{ and } \frac{3}{30}$$

$$\frac{41}{30}$$

Answer: 1 and $\frac{11}{30}$

3. What is two and a quarter plus one and seven eighths?

Always add (or subtract) whole numbers first.

Then find the lowest denominator for the fractions. When the parts of each fraction are added, the result is nine parts. As eight parts are required to make each unit, the nine parts produces one unit with one part left over.

The extra unit is added to the original whole numbers.

$$2\frac{1}{4} + 1\frac{7}{8}$$

$$= 3\frac{1}{4} + \frac{7}{8} = 3\frac{9}{8}$$

Answer: $4\frac{1}{8}$

4. Take 3 and $\frac{2}{3}$ from 5 and $\frac{1}{2}$

Take away the whole numbers first. Then find the lowest common denominator for the two fractions.

You cannot take four sixths from three sixths. Therefore, you take a whole number and turn it into sixths, adding these to the two parts you have already. 4 from 9 leaves 5.

The answer is one and five sixths.

$$5\frac{1}{2} - 3\frac{2}{3}$$

$$= 2\frac{3}{6} - \frac{4}{6}$$

$$= 1\frac{9}{6} - \frac{4}{6}$$

Answer: $1\frac{5}{6}$

5. What is $1\frac{1}{2} - 2\frac{1}{3} + 1\frac{1}{4}$?

Add or subtract the whole numbers figures first. Then find the lowest common denominator in order to be able to add or subtract the number of parts.

$$1\frac{1}{2} - 2\frac{1}{3} + 1\frac{1}{4}$$

$$= 1\frac{6}{12} - 2\frac{4}{12} + 1\frac{3}{12}$$

$$= \frac{6}{12} - \frac{4}{12} + \frac{3}{12}$$

Answer: $\frac{5}{12}$

How to multiply and divide fractions

1. What is $\frac{2}{5}$ of 80?

Remember that 'of' always means multiply. Multiply the top numbers (the numerators) together, then multiply the bottom numbers (the denominators) together. Divide the 'top heavy' (or improper) fraction by the bottom number.

$$\frac{2}{5} \times \frac{80}{1} = \frac{160}{5} = 32$$

Answer: 32

2. What is $3\frac{3}{5} \times 4\frac{1}{4}$?

Change mixed fractions (whole numbers and parts) to improper fractions by multiplying the whole number by the denominator, then adding the numerator. Multiply the numerators together then multiply the denominators together. Change into a proper fraction by dividing the denominator into the numerator. Reduce the fraction to its lowest terms.

$$3\frac{3}{5} \times 4\frac{1}{4}$$

$$= \frac{18}{5} \times \frac{17}{4}$$

$$= \frac{306}{20} = 15\frac{6}{20}$$

Answer: $15\frac{3}{10}$

3. What is $2\frac{1}{2}$ of $3\frac{2}{5}$?

By following the instructions above, go through the process required to arrive at the answer of $8\frac{1}{2}$

$$2\frac{1}{2} \text{ of } 3\frac{2}{5}$$

Answer: $8\frac{1}{2}$

4. What is $\frac{3}{5} \div \frac{1}{2}$?

To divide a fraction, first turn the right hand fraction upside down (invert the fraction).
Then proceed as with multiplication, multiplying the numerators and denominators, then dividing one into the other.

$$\frac{3}{5} \div \frac{1}{2}$$

$$= \frac{3}{5} \times \frac{2}{1}$$

$$= \frac{6}{5}$$

Answer: $1\frac{1}{5}$

5. What is $4\frac{1}{4} \div 2\frac{1}{4}$?

With mixed fractions, convert the whole numbers into units and add to the existing numerators.
Invert the right hand fraction. Proceed as for multiplication.
Reduce large numbers where possible to their simplest terms. In this case by dividing both numerator and denominator by 2.
When no further reduction is possible divide denominator into numerator.

$$4\frac{1}{4} \div 2\frac{1}{4}$$

$$= \frac{17}{4} \div \frac{9}{4} = \frac{17}{4} \times \frac{4}{9}$$

$$= \frac{68}{36} = \frac{34}{18} = \frac{17}{9}$$

Answer: $1\frac{8}{9}$

How to work with percentages

1. What is 20% of 40?

'Per cent' is the same as saying 'out of a hundred' or 'per hundred' or by using the symbol '%'.
In this case the question is what are 20 hundredths of 40. 20% is one fifth. Then, to find one fifth of 40, divide by 5.
A quick way to do percentages is to use 10 per cent. Thus, 10% is one tenth of 100%. Therefore, in this case, 10% or one tenth of 40 is 4. 20% would be twice this figure, which is 8.

$$20\% = \frac{20}{100} = \frac{1}{5}$$

$^{40}/_5$

Answer: 8

2. What is 24% as a fraction?
Simply place the percentage over a
hundred. Then reduce both the
denominator and the numerator equally
until you cannot break it down any further.
In this case, both parts were divided (or
cancelled) by 2 and then 2 again. No other
number can be divided into both 6 and
25, so this fraction has reached the lowest
common denominator.

$$24\% = \frac{24}{100} = \frac{12}{50} = \frac{6}{25}$$

Answer: $\frac{6}{25}$

3. What is 12½% as a fraction?
Fractions in the numerator are eliminated
by multiplying by the denominator and
adding the part of the numerator. In this
case, 2 by 12 is 24, add 1 is 25.
As the numerator has been multiplied by
2, so the denominator has to be multiplied
by 2.
The fraction can now be reduced (or
cancelled) using 5.

$$12\frac{1}{2}\% = \frac{12\frac{1}{2}}{100} = \frac{25}{200} = \frac{1}{8}$$

Answer: $\frac{1}{8}$

4. Change $\frac{5}{16}$ to a percentage

To change a fraction to a percentage you
multiply by 100%.
The resulting fraction can be cancelled
by 4. Dividing the numerator by the
denominator results in a decimal
percentage or another, correct answer,
31¼%.

$$\frac{5}{16} \times \frac{100}{1}$$
$$= \frac{500}{16}$$
$$= \frac{125}{4}$$

Answer: 31.25%

5. What is a 40% reduction on an item
costing £240.00?
Another way is to say that 10%, that is,
one tenth, of £240 is £24. So, 40% is 24
by 4, which is £96.

$$40\% = \frac{40}{100} = 0.4$$
$$0.4 \times 240$$

Answer: £96

Money

1. What is the total of £16.09, £23.68 and £21.89?

Most money systems are in decimals to which all the normal operations (addition, subtraction, division and multiplication) apply. This applies equally well to currencies such as the pound, the dollar and the euro.

$$16.09$$
$$+23.68$$
$$+21.89$$
$$\overline{61.66}$$

Answer: £61.66

2. What is 10% of £61.66?

The decimal system makes it easy to work in percentages. In this case, it is simple to move the decimal point one space.

$$£61.66 \times \frac{10}{100}$$

Answer: £6.166
(£6.17)

3. If £61.66 has to be shared equally by three people, how much does each person receive?

When a fraction cannot be divided exactly into a decimal a recurring figure, in this case 3, results. This has to be 'corrected' to a given number of places of decimals. In this case, as we are dealing with money, it would be corrected to two places. In engineering calculations, several places of decimals might be necessary.

$$£61.66 \times \frac{1}{3} = 20.55333$$

Answer: £20.55

4. If the rate of the euro is 1 pound = 1.25 euros, how many euros will be obtained for £50?

50×1.25 or 5×12.5 or $\frac{1}{2} \times 125 = 62.5$

1 pound = 1.25 euros
10 = 12.5
100 = 125
Answer: 62.50 euros

Graphs and tables

A graph is a pictorial representation of numerical information making it much easier to perceive the significant differences between numerical relationships.

1. The graph shows average rainfall in millimetres (mm) for the first six months of the year.

Visual inspection of the graph enables the trend to be readily observed.

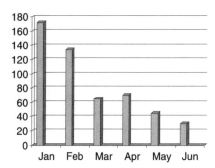

Which was the wettest month?

Answer: January

2. From the chart below, what was the percentage of rainfall in June compared with January?

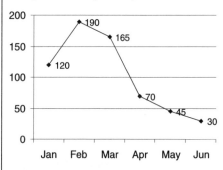

This type of graph is called a line graph.

$$\frac{30}{120} \times \frac{100}{1}$$

Answer: 25%

3. From the chart below, what was the driest month?

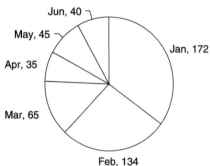

Jun, 40
May, 45
Apr, 35
Mar, 65
Jan, 172
Feb, 134

This type of chart is used to show how much of a total a certain part represents. It is less easy to see a trend than in a line or bar graph.

Answer: April

4. A table is a collection of relevant information, ordered in such a way as to enable you to perceive the significant connections between and within a certain, related set.

From the table below, how many examination candidates failed to get the pass mark of 50 on Test B?

Test

	A	B	C	D	E
John	25	45	55	95	40
Mary	45	55	45	35	80
Susan	15	25	60	50	60
Sam	65	35	75	70	30

Answer: 3

5. If all the tests were out of a maximum of 100, who got more than 50% on Test A?   Answer: Sam

6. If the pass mark on each test is 50, how many candidates passed three or more tests?   Answer: 2

7. What was the hardest test for the candidates?
The hardest must be the one on which the candidates obtained the lowest marks overall. This is 150 on Test A.   Answer: Test A

Space

1. What is the area of the rectangle below?

3.5 cm

2 cm

To find the area, that is, the surface of a rectangle or any other 'right-sided' figure, such as a square, multiply one side by the other. Sometimes this is described as 'width by length' or 'length by height'. Be careful to label the answer correctly.

$3.5 \times 2 = 7$

Answer: 7 square cm

2. What is the volume of the figure below?

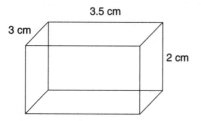

Volume is found by multiplying the base area (in a right-sided figure any side may be the base) by the height. In this case, we already know the area of one side, but it is easy to find the area of any side.

vol = base area × height
= 7 × 3
= 21
or
vol = 2 × 3.5 × 3
= 21
Answer: 21 cubic cm

3. What is the length of a side of a rectangle if its volume is 24 cubic (cu) cm and its width is 2 cm and its height is 3 cm?

24 = length × 2 × 3
24 = length × 6
$\frac{24}{6}$ = length

Answer: 4 cm

4. What is the perimeter of the rectangle below?

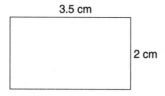

'Perimeter' means 'around the outside'. Simply add the length or 'distance' of all the sides together.

Answer: 11 cm

5. What is the volume of the figure below?

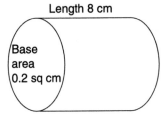

Length 8 cm

Base
area
0.2 sq cm

The rule already given for volume is 'base times height', which applies to any regular figure even though the base may be circular.

Answer: 1.6 cu cm

Applied tests

In Part 2 you will find out your likely suitability for certain types of study or work, either immediately or after a period of training.

Test 1: Number usage

In this book:

+ means add or plus
− means subtract or take away
* or × means multiply or times
/ or ÷ means divide.

In this test you have to add, subtract, multiply and divide. You are given a sum and you have to write the answer in the space provided.

Do not mark the book if it is not your own, write your answers on a separate sheet instead. You will need paper and a pen or pencil for any working out you want to do. Using a calculator is not allowed.

The first example has been done for you.

Example 1

What is the sum of 23 + 49 + 88?　　　Answer:　　　$\boxed{160}$

Example 2

A football stadium holds thirty thousand
people, but attendance on a certain day
was only fifteen thousand and eighty
nine. How many seats were unfilled?　　Answer:　　$\boxed{}$

Example 3

Divide 247 by 13　　　　　　　　　　Answer:　　$\boxed{}$

Answers and explanation

This is how you may have set out Example 1:

$$\begin{array}{r} 23 \\ +\,49 \\ +\,88 \\ \hline 160 \end{array}$$

Answer:　$\boxed{160}$

This is how you may have set out Example 2:

$$\begin{array}{r} 30000 \\ -15089 \\ \hline 14911 \end{array}$$

Answer:　$\boxed{14911}$

This is how you may have set out Example 3:

$$\begin{array}{r} 19 \\ 13\overline{)247} \\ 13 \\ \hline 117 \end{array}$$

Answer:　$\boxed{19}$

Make sure you have sufficient spare paper before you start the test. Write your answer in the space provided or on a separate sheet if you should not mark this book. Using a calculator is not allowed.

Timed test: 15 minutes. Power test: 45 minutes.

1. 14 plus 9   Answer: _____

2. 46 + 35   Answer: _____

3. 54 + 76 + 113   Answer: _____

4. 29 – 11   Answer: _____

5. 98 + 76 – 83   Answer: _____

6. One hundred and fourteen and one
    thousand and six   Answer: _____

7. 386 – 297 + 409   Answer: _____

8. What is the difference between 604
    and 313?   Answer: _____

9. 6006 – 689   Answer: _____

10. 7 times 9   Answer: _____

11. 59 * 5   Answer: _____

12. 369 * 8   Answer: _____

13. 49 * 23   Answer: _____

14. 483 * 27   Answer: _____

15. How many fives are there in sixty five?   Answer: _____

16. 200/8   Answer: _____

17. 336/14   Answer: _____

18. 364/13   Answer: _____

19. 874/19   Answer: _____

20. 1806/43   Answer: _____

21. 400 * 600   Answer: _____

22.   2400/40   Answer: [   ]

23.   27 – 31 – 13 + 43 – 62   Answer: [   ]

24.   A salesman travels around 1300 miles
      each calendar month. How many miles
      does he probably travel each year?   Answer: [   ]

25.   On a certain day, a sweet factory
      produced 5609 chocolates. These were
      placed in boxes of 24 to a box, then in
      cases of five boxes to a case. How many
      cases were filled, how many boxes were
      left over and how many odd chocolates
      remained?   Answer: [   ]

26.   What number comes next after the
      number 31 in the sequence?
      3   10   17   24   31   ?   Answer: [   ]

27.   What is the missing number in this
      sequence?
      8   16   32   64   ?   256   Answer: [   ]

28.   What is next in the sequence after the
      number 6?
      162   54   18   6   ?   Answer: [   ]

29.   What is the missing number?
      120   108   97   ?   78   70   Answer: [   ]

30.   What is next in the sequence after –1?
      –9   –7   –5   –3   –1   ?   Answer: [   ]

Answers to Test 1

1. 23	11. 295	21. 240,000
2. 81	12. 2,952	22. 60
3. 243	13. 1,127	23. −36
4. 18	14. 13,041	24. 15,600
5. 91	15. 13	25. 46, 3, 17
6. 1,120	16. 25	26. 38
7. 498	17. 24	27. 128
8. 291	18. 28	28. 2
9. 5,317	19. 46	29. 87
10. 63	20. 42	30. 1

Conversion of scores on Test 1

Test score = number correct minus errors = _____

	Below average				Average		Above average			
Timed score	1	2	3–4	5–6	7–9	10–12	13–16	17–20	21–24	25+
Power score		1–3	4–7	8–12	13–16	17–20	21–23	24–26	27–28	29+
Score out of ten	1	2	3	4	5	6	7	8	9	10

Test 2: Proportion

In this book:

+ means add or plus
− means subtract or take away
* or × means multiply or times
/ or ÷ means divide

In this test you have to add, subtract, multiply and divide decimals, fractions and percentages. You are given a sum and you have to write the answer in the space provided. Using a calculator is not allowed. You will need paper and a pen or pencil for any working out you want to do. Do not mark the book if it is not your own, write your answers on a separate sheet instead.

The first example has been done for you.

Example 1

What is $\frac{7}{10}$ written as a decimal?   Answer: | 0.7 |

Example 2

Which is the larger fraction, $\frac{2}{4}$ or $\frac{3}{4}$?   Answer: | |

Example 3

What is 15% as a fraction?   Answer: | |

Answers and explanation

Example 1 is solved by dividing the bottom figure into the top. There are seven units, but 10 into 7 will not go, so a zero is added from the next column to make 70 parts. You can now divide 10 into 70, being careful to place the decimal point before the 7.

Answer: | 0.7 |

In Example 2, the common denominator is 12 (3 × 4), therefore

$$\frac{2}{3} \text{ or } \frac{3}{4} = \frac{8}{12} \text{ or } \frac{9}{12}$$

Thus, $\frac{9}{12}$ is larger and the answer is $\frac{3}{4}$ Answer: | 3/4 |

This is how you may have set out Example 3:

$15\% = \frac{15}{100} = \frac{3}{20}$ by cancelling by 5   Answer: | 3/20 |

Before you start the test make sure you have sufficient spare paper for any working out you want to do. Write your answer in the space provided or on a separate sheet if you should not mark this book.

Timed test: 15 minutes. Power test: 45 minutes.

1. Change $\frac{2}{5}$ to a decimal   Answer:

2. Which is larger, $\frac{1}{4}$ or $\frac{1}{3}$?   Answer:

3. Change 30% to a fraction   Answer:

4. Change $\frac{36}{100}$ to a decimal   Answer:

5. Which is larger, $\frac{3}{2}$ or $\frac{13}{8}$ or $\frac{8}{5}$?   Answer:

6. Change $\frac{3}{4}$ to a percentage   Answer:

7. Change $\frac{509}{100}$ to a decimal   Answer:

8. $\frac{3}{8} + \frac{1}{4}$ Answer:

9. Change 95% to a decimal   Answer:

10. 2.4 + 3.7 + 4.9   Answer:

11. $\frac{1}{8} + \frac{1}{3}$ Answer:

12. Change 17½% to a decimal   Answer:

13. 3.07 + 7.1 + 50.009   Answer:

14. $\frac{2}{3} - \frac{1}{4}$ Answer:

15. Change $\frac{12}{25}$ to a percentage   Answer:

16. 48.02 − 7.3   Answer:

17. $1\frac{5}{8} - 1\frac{3}{5}$ Answer:

18. Change $\frac{17}{40}$ to a percentage   Answer: [   ]

19. 1.06 × 2.74   Answer: [   ]

20. $\frac{2}{3} \times \frac{5}{6}$ Answer: [   ]

21. Change 0.81 to a percentage   Answer: [   ]

22. 5.6 ÷ 4   Answer: [   ]

23. $\frac{3}{4} \div \frac{1}{3}$ Answer: [   ]

24. What is $18\frac{3}{4}$ as a percentage of 25?   Answer: [   ]

25. 6.79 ÷ 0.07   Answer: [   ]

26. $1\frac{7}{8} \times 4\frac{1}{5}$ Answer: [   ]

27. 24% of £10.50   Answer: [   ]

28. 1.3363 ÷ 0.0023   Answer: [   ]

29. $4\frac{3}{8} \div 1\frac{1}{2}$ Answer: [   ]

30. What does an article cost if reduced
    from £96 by 45%?   Answer:

Answers to Test 2

1. 0.4
2. $\frac{1}{3}$
3. $\frac{3}{10}$
4. 0.36
5. $\frac{13}{8}$
6. 75%
7. 5.09
8. $\frac{5}{8}$
9. 0.95
10. 11

11. $\frac{11}{24}$
12. 0.175
13. 60.179
14. $\frac{5}{12}$
15. 30%
16. 40.72
17. $\frac{1}{40}$
18. 42.5 (42½)%
19. 2.9044
20. $\frac{5}{9}$

21. 81%
22. 1.4
23. $2\frac{1}{4}$
24. 75%
25. 97
26. $7\frac{7}{8}$ (7.875)
27. £2.52
28. 581
29. $2\frac{11}{12}$
30. £52.80

Conversion of scores on Test 2

Test score = number correct minus errors = _____

		Below average			Average		Above average			
Timed score	1	2	3–4	5–7	8–11	12–15	16–19	20–22	23–24	25+
Power score		1–3	4–7	8–12	13–16	17–20	21–23	24–26	27–28	29+
Score out of ten	1	2	3	4	5	6	7	8	9	10

Test 3: Money

In this test you are given a sum and you have to write the answer in the space provided.

Using a calculator is not allowed. You will need paper and a pen or pencil for any working out you want to do. Do not mark the book if it is not your own, write your answers on a separate sheet instead.

The first example has been done for you.

Example 1

What is £4.56 and £6.49?   Answer: £11.05

Example 2

A person was paid a monthly wage of
£2,600 but was deducted £545.08 for tax
and insurance. How much was left?   Answer:

Example 3

A painting was bought for £150 and sold
later for £165. What was the percentage
profit?   Answer:

Answers and explanation

The answer to Example 1 can be worked out as:

$$\begin{array}{r} 4.56 \\ +6.49 \\ \hline 11.05 \end{array}$$

Answer: 11.05

In Example 2 the sum is:

$$\begin{array}{r} 2600.00 \\ -545.08 \\ \hline 2054.92 \end{array}$$

Answer: 2054.92

In Example 3, the profit of £15 on the price of £150 is 10%.

In this book:

+ means add or plus
− means subtract or take away
* or × means multiply or times
/ or ÷ means divide.

Make sure you have sufficient spare paper before you start the test. Write your answer in the space provided or on a separate sheet to prevent marking this book.

Timed test: 15 minutes. Power test: 45 minutes.

1. £2.60 + £1.40   Answer: [   ]

2. £6.37 + £4.06   Answer: [   ]

3. £10.09 + £0.99   Answer: [   ]

4. £20.86 + £33.92 + £41.07   Answer: [   ]

5. £4 – £3.50   Answer: [   ]

6. £9.27 – £4.78   Answer: [   ]

7. £10 – £6.90   Answer: [   ]

8. £85.92 – £61.79   Answer: [   ]

9. £5.43 × 4   Answer: [   ]

10. £1056.5 × 12   Answer: [   ]

11. £224.64/24   Answer: [   ]

12. What is the cost per quarter if the
    annual cost is £997?   Answer: [   ]

13. A man works a 40-hour week at £8.40
    per hour. What is his weekly wage?   Answer: [   ]

14. A television set is for sale at £499 or a
    deposit of £50 and 11 monthly payments
    of £44.99. How much extra is repaid?   Answer: [   ]

15. A bank offers a loan of £1,000 to be repaid
    with 12 monthly payments of 'only' £95 a
    month. How much extra is paid back?   Answer: [   ]

16. What is the percentage profit on the loan
    in question 15?   Answer: [   ]

17. If an item is bought for £80 and resold to
    make a 30% profit, what is its sale price?   Answer: [   ]

18. A car costs £22,000, which can be
     purchased with an initial charge of £3,856
     and the balance in 24 equal monthly
     instalments. What is the cost of each
     monthly instalment?   Answer: _____

19. What is paid for an item reduced by
     37½% from £360?   Answer: _____

20. What is the basic salary of a managing
     director if his bonus of £30,000 (thirty
     thousand) is 25% of his annual salary?   Answer: _____

21. A sales executive is paid £20,000 per
     annum plus 7½% commission on his
     sales of machinery. What did he earn in
     total last year if his sales were £500,000
     (half a million pounds)?   Answer: _____

22. What is the percentage profit or loss if the
     buying price of an item is £180 and the
     selling price is £189?   Answer: _____

23. What is the percentage profit or loss if an
     item is sold for £83.20 that was purchased
     for £64?   Answer: _____

24. What was the cost of an item that made a
     12½% loss when sold for £56?   Answer: _____

25. If the annual interest on savings is 5.4%,
     how much is earned on savings of £400?   Answer: _____

26. A bank loan is 11% a year on £3,000.
     How much interest is paid?   Answer: _____

27. What is the total cost if repairs to a car
     are £120 plus tax of 17.5%?   Answer: _____

28. What will a £150 item cost after tax at
     17.5% is added?   Answer: _____

29. What is the discount price of 15 % on
     £165?   Answer: _____

30. What is a 15% deposit on furniture
     costing £2,700?   Answer: _____

Answers to Test 3

1.	£4	11.	£9.36	21.	£57,500
2.	£10.43	12.	£249.25	22.	5%
3.	£11.08	13.	£336	23.	30%
4.	£95.85	14.	£45.89	24.	£64
5.	£0.50	15.	£140	25.	£21.60
6.	£4.49	16.	14%	26.	£330
7.	£3.10	17.	£104	27.	£141
8.	£24.13	18.	£756	28.	£176.25
9.	£21.72	19.	£225	29.	£140.25
10.	£12,678	20.	£120,000	30.	£405

Conversion of scores on Test 3

Test score = number correct minus errors = _____

	Below average				Average		Above average			
Timed score	1	2	3–4	5–7	8–11	12–15	16–19	20–22	23–24	25+
Power score	1–2	3–5	6–11	12–16	17–19	20–21	22–23	24–25	26–27	28+
Score out of ten	1	2	3	4	5	6	7	8	9	10

Test 4: Graphs and tables

In this test you are given a sum and you have to write the answer in the space provided. You will need paper and a pen or pencil for any working out. Calculators are not allowed. Do not mark the book if it is not your own, but write your answers on a separate sheet.

The first example has been done for you.

Example 1

The graph shows the average height in metres of boys and girls in a certain school between the ages of 10 and 18 years.

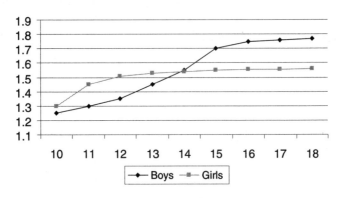

1a. At what age were the boys about
    1.4 metres tall?   Answer: [   ]

1b. At what age were the boys and girls almost
    exactly the same height?   Answer: [   ]

1c. At age 18, approximately how much taller
    are the boys than the girls?   Answer: [   ]

Example 2

The table below shows attendance at four football clubs on certain dates.

	Liverpool	Arsenal	Chelsea	Newcastle	Total
January 27	31,396	44,696	47,065	34,663	157,820
February 3	24,497	35,465	38,998	27,654	126,614
February 10	33,073	39,677	43,655		151,805
February 17	34,987	46,765	49,765	37,650	169,167
Club total	123,953	166,603		135,367	605,406

2a. Which date was least well attended?   Answer: [   ]

2b. Which club had the highest attendance
in total?   Answer: [   ]

2c. What is the correct figure for attendance
at Newcastle on February 10?   Answer: [   ]

Answers and explanation

1a. 12½
At 12 years the line for the boys is below the
1.4 metre point and at 13 years has gone above it.

1b. 14
The two graph lines cross at age 14.

1c. 0.2
At age 18 the girls are almost 1.6 and the boys
almost 1.8 metres tall.

2a. February 3
The lowest total is 126,614, which is on February 3.

2b. Chelsea
Among the clubs, Chelsea had the highest attendance
of 179,483.

2c. 35,400
The sum is 135,367 – 34,663 – 27,654 – 37,650
= 35,400.

Make sure you have sufficient spare paper before you start the
test. Write your answer in the space provided or on a separate
sheet if you should not mark this book.

Timed test: 15 minutes. Power test: 45 minutes.

1.   The graph shows how quickly a bicycle and a truck accelerate.

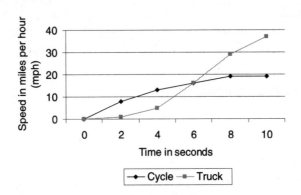

   a) What speed is the truck doing after
       8 seconds?   Answer: ⬚

   b) How long does it take for the truck to
       reach the same speed as the bicycle?   Answer: ⬚

   c) How long does it take for the bicycle
       to reach its maximum speed?   Answer: ⬚

   d) After 10 seconds, approximately how
       much faster is the truck going than the
       cyclist?   Answer: ⬚

2.   The graph shows the exchange rate of dollars to pounds.

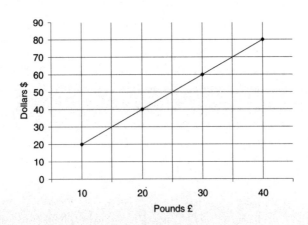

a) How much is a pound worth in dollars? Answer: [ ]

b) How much is 50 dollars worth in
   pounds?   Answer: [ ]

c) How many dollars will be obtained
   from 27 pounds?   Answer: [ ]

d) A watch costs £28 in London and $69
   in New York. What is the difference
   in pounds?   Answer: [ ]

3. The following bus timetable is of three buses
   leaving every 40 minutes.

Bus station	09.00	09.40	10.20
Town hall	09.05	09.45	10.25
The Mall	09.21	10.01	10.41
Waterside	09.31	10.11	10.48
East Side	09.52	10.32	11.09
Compton	10.29	11.09	11.46
Park Street	10.36	11.16	11.49
Docks	10.45	11.25	11.55
Terminus	10.59	11.39	12.01

a) How long does the 09.00 bus take
   from the bus station to the terminus?   Answer: [ ]

b) How long does the 10.20 bus take
   from the bus station to the terminus?   Answer: [ ]

c) On the 10.20 bus, how long is the
   longest journey between stops?   Answer: [ ]

d) How long will it take to get from
   Waterside to Park Street on the 10.20
   bus?   Answer: [ ]

e) How long will the same journey take
   on the 09.40 bus?   Answer: [ ]

f) If I just miss the 10.32 at East Side, how
   long will I have to wait for the next bus? Answer: [ ]

4. The graph shows the journey of a delivery vehicle.

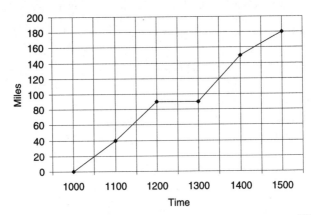

a) How many hours did the journey take?   Answer:

b) How many miles were covered in the
   second hour of the journey?   Answer:

c) How many miles were travelled
   between 12 and 1 pm?   Answer:

d) What was the average speed of the
   vehicle between 1 and 2 pm?   Answer:

e) What was the average speed for the
   journey?   Answer:

f) What would have been the average
   speed if there had been no stop?   Answer:

5. The table shows the distance in miles
   between cities in England and Scotland.

Distances given in miles	Dover	Leeds	London	Oxford	Perth	Sheffield
Leeds	260		188	163	234	34
London	76	188		57	413	159
Oxford	133	163	57		396	129
Perth	485	234	413	396		267
Sheffield	234	34	159	129	267	

a) How far is it between Oxford and
   Sheffield?   Answer: [   ]

b) If I go from Dover to London and then to
   Oxford, how many miles would this journey
   be in total?   Answer: [   ]

c) How long would it take to get from Leeds to
   Perth at an average speed of 60 miles
   per hour?   Answer: [   ]

d) What is the average speed of a motorist
   who takes 3 hours to get from Sheffield to
   London?   Answer: [   ]

e) What is the average speed of a motorist
   who takes 40 minutes to get from Sheffield
   to Leeds?   Answer: [   ]

6.   A family calculated their average monthly spending as follows.

a) How much is spent on 'food and home'? Answer: [   ]

b) How much is spent on the two highest
   bills?   Answer: [   ]

c) How much is spent in total per month?   Answer: [   ]

d) What percentage of the total is spent on
   'car and travel'?   Answer: [   ]

e) How much is spent on 'entertainment' as
   a fraction of the whole?   Answer: [   ]

Answers to Test 4

1. a) 30 mph
   b) 6 seconds
   c) 8 seconds
   d) 20 mph
2. a) 2
   b) 25
   c) 54
   d) £6.50
3. a) 1 hour,
      59 minutes
   b) 1 hour,
      41 minutes

   c) 37 minutes
   d) 1 hour,
      1 minute
   e) 1 hour,
      5 minutes
   f) 37 minutes
4. a) 5 hours
   b) 45
   c) 0
   d) 60 mph
   e) 36 mph
   f) 45

5. a) 129
   b) 133
   c) 3 hours,
      54 minutes
   d) 53 mph
   e) 51 mph
6. a) £550
   b) £1,350
   c) £2,400
   d) 12.5%
   e) $\dfrac{1}{12}$

Conversion of scores on Test 4

Test score = number correct minus errors = _____

	Below average				Average		Above average			
Timed score	1	2	3–4	5–7	8–11	12–14	15–17	18–21	22–25	26+
Power score	1	2	3	4–7	8–12	13–18	19–22	23–26	27–28	29+
Score out of ten	1	2	3	4	5	6	7	8	9	10

Test 5: Space

In this test you have to calculate the size and volume of different shapes. You have to write the answer in the space provided. You will need paper and a pen or pencil for doing rough drawings of the problems you are given, as well as for any working out. Using a calculator is not allowed. Do not mark the book if it is not your own, but do your rough work and record your answers on a separate sheet.

The first example has been done for you.

Example 1

5 cm

2 cm

What is the total length (perimeter) of the sides of
this rectangle?   Answer: 14 cm

What is the area of this rectangle?   Answer:

Example 2

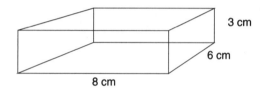

3 cm

6 cm

8 cm

What is the volume of this box?   Answer:

Answers and explanation

In Example 1, the length of the sides (the perimeter) is the total
of all the sides together, so the answer is 14 cm, because 5 + 5 + 2
+ 2 = 14.

In the second question, the area of the rectangle is 10 square
cm, because 5 × 2 = 10.

In Example 2, the volume is given by area of the base × height.
The area of the base is 8 × 6 = 48. The height is 3 cm, so the
volume is 48 × 3 = 144 (or 144 cu cm or 144³).

Make sure you have sufficient spare paper before you start the
test. Write your answer in the space provided or on a separate
sheet if you should not mark this book.

Timed test: 15 minutes. Power test: 45 minutes.

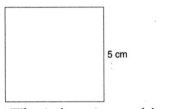

(a)

1.   What is the perimeter of the square in Figure (a)?   Answer:

2.   What is the area of Figure (a)?   Answer:

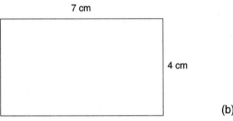

(b)

3.   What is the length of the short side of Figure (b) if one side is 7 cm and the perimeter is 22 cm?   Answer:

4.   What is the area of Figure (b)?   Answer:

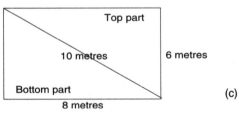

(c)

5.   A 10-metre line divides a rectangle into two parts as shown in Figure (c). What is the length of the perimeter around the bottom part?   Answer:

6.   What is the area of the top part of the rectangle?   Answer:

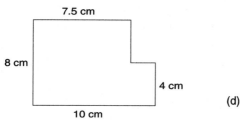

7. What is the length of the perimeter of
   Figure (d)?

   Answer: _____

8. What is the area of Figure (d)?

   Answer: _____

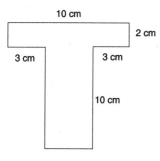

9. What is the total length of the perimeter
   of Figure (e)?

   Answer: _____

10. What is the area of Figure (e)?

    Answer: _____

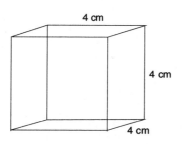

11. If a cube, Figure (f) has a side of 4 cm,
     what is the surface area of the cube?   Answer: [   ]

12. What is the volume of the cube in
     Figure (f)?   Answer: [   ]

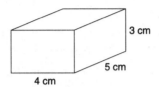

(g)

13. What is the area of the base of
     Figure (g)?   Answer: [   ]

14. What is the volume of Figure (g)?   Answer: [   ]

3 metres

4.5 metres

3.5 metres

5 metres   (h)

15. What is the area of a floor, as shown in
     Figure (h)?   Answer: [   ]

16. How many 50 cm square tiles will be
     needed to cover the floor?   Answer: [   ]

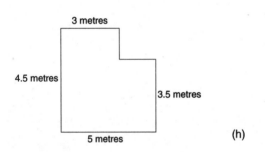

(i)

17. What is the length around the outside, shaded face of Figure (i)?   Answer: [   ]

18. What is the volume of the figure?   Answer: [   ]

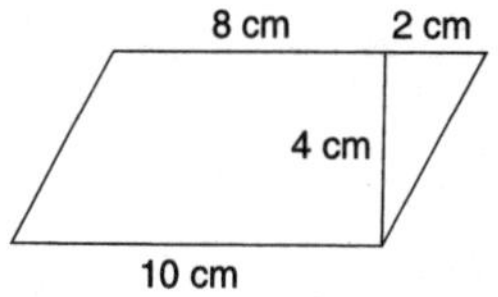

8 cm   2 cm

4 cm

10 cm

(j)

19. What is the area of Figure (j)?   Answer: [   ]

20. What is the area of the triangle in Figure (j)?   Answer: [   ]

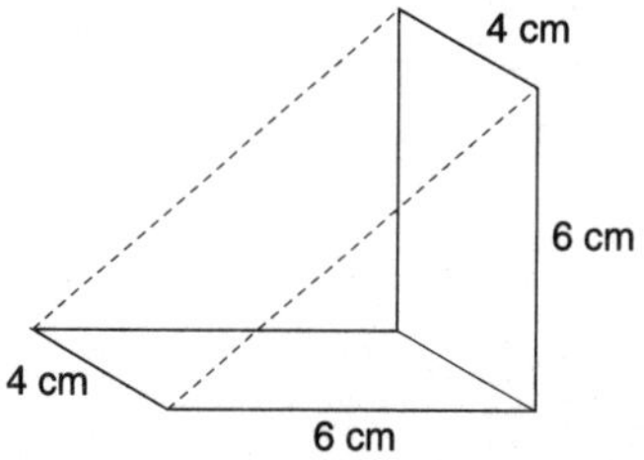

4 cm

6 cm

4 cm

6 cm

(k)

21. What is the surface area of Figure (k) less the sloping area?   Answer: [   ]

22. What is the volume of Figure (k)?   Answer: [   ]

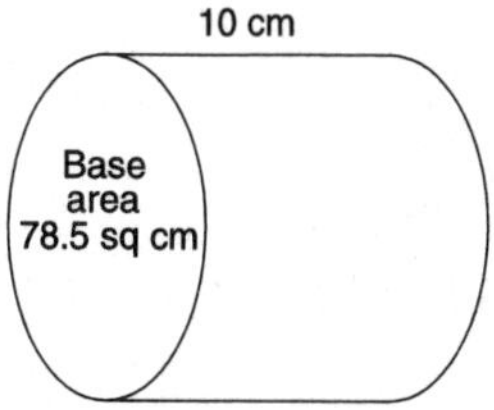

10 cm

Base area 78.5 sq cm

(l)

23. The circumference of the can in Figure (l) is 31.4 cm. What is the area of the side of the can?   Answer: [   ]

24. What is the volume of the can?   Answer: [   ]

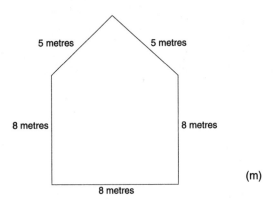

(m)

25. What is the area of the side of a house, total height 11 metres, as shown in Figure (m)?   Answer:

26. A can of paint costs £15 and covers 10 square metres. How much will it cost to buy enough cans of paint to cover the side of the house in Figure (m)?   Answer:

4 metres

3 metres

(n)

27. How many floorboards 4.2 metres long × 0.12 metres wide will be needed to cover the floor shown in Figure (n)?   Answer:

28. How many square metres of floorboard will be wasted?   Answer:

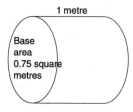

1 metre

Base area 0.75 square metres

(o)

29. The container in Figure (o) has a base area of 0.75 square metres and a length of 1 metre. What is its volume?   Answer: [ ]

30. If the container is full of liquid, how many bottles of 0.0003 cubic metres can be filled from it?   Answer: [ ]

Answers to Test 5

1. 20 cm	11. 96 sq cm	21. 84 sq cm
2. 25 sq cm	12. 64 cu cm	22. 72 cu cm
3. 4 cm	13. 20 sq cm	23. 314 sq cm
4. 28 sq cm	14. 60 cu cm	24. 785 cu cm
5. 24 m	15. 20.5 sq m	25. 76 sq m
6. 24 sq m	16. 82	26. £120
7. 36 cm	17. 40 cm	27. 25
8. 70 sq cm	18. 624 cu cm	28. 0.6 sq m
9. 44 cm	19. 40 sq cm	29. 0.75 cu m
10. 60 sq cm	20. 4 sq cm	30. 2,500

Conversion of scores on Test 5

Test score = number correct minus errors = _____

	Below average				Average		Above average			
Timed score	1	2	3–4	5–6	7–9	10–12	13–15	16–18	19–21	22+
Power score	1	2–3	4–7	8–12	13–16	17–20	21–22	23–24	25–26	27+
Score out of ten	1	2	3	4	5	6	7	8	9	10

Test 6: Accuracy

This test evaluates how well you maintain your concentration on a checking task. Each question provides you with six numbers. You have to decide which are the highest and lowest numbers. Tick the box alongside the letters that are your answers.

Example

		Highest	Lowest
a)	30661	☐	☐
b)	31660	☐	☐
c)	21667	☐	☑
d)	32616	☑	☐
e)	31760	☐	☐

In the example, the highest number is 32616. Therefore d) has been ticked to indicate the correct answer. The number 21667 is the lowest. Therefore c) has been given as the answer. The full and correct answer to the example is 'd c'.

Do not mark this book if it is not yours, but record your answers on a separate sheet of paper.

It is important to work quickly and accurately. Work down the page completing the questions in order.

Timed test: 10 minutes. Power test: 20 minutes.

1.		Highest	Lowest
a)	601	☐	☐
b)	709	☐	☐
c)	806	☐	☐
d)	339	☐	☐
e)	455	☐	☐
f)	345	☐	☐

2.		Highest	Lowest
a)	233	☐	☐
b)	253	☐	☐
c)	352	☐	☐
d)	235	☐	☐
e)	223	☐	☐
f)	303	☐	☐

3.		Highest	Lowest
a)	7173	☐	☐
b)	7713	☐	☐
c)	7317	☐	☐
d)	7731	☐	☐
e)	7377	☐	☐
f)	7113	☐	☐

4.

		Highest	Lowest
a)	6081	☐	☐
b)	6794	☐	☐
c)	6543	☐	☐
d)	6415	☐	☐
e)	6406	☐	☐
f)	6472	☐	☐

5.

		Highest	Lowest
a)	68713	☐	☐
b)	68901	☐	☐
c)	68840	☐	☐
d)	68732	☐	☐
e)	68712	☐	☐
f)	68932	☐	☐

6.

		Highest	Lowest
a)	550987	☐	☐
b)	551789	☐	☐
c)	550678	☐	☐
d)	550146	☐	☐
e)	551432	☐	☐
f)	550499	☐	☐

7.   Highest Lowest
a)   10121211   ☐   ☐
b)   10212112   ☐   ☐
c)   10201112   ☐   ☐
d)   10002221   ☐   ☐
e)   10211112   ☐   ☐
f)   10101010   ☐   ☐

8.   Highest Lowest
a)   435534   ☐   ☐
b)   334554   ☐   ☐
c)   434543   ☐   ☐
d)   335454   ☐   ☐
e)   334545   ☐   ☐
f)   434554   ☐   ☐

9.   Highest Lowest
a)   711867   ☐   ☐
b)   765432   ☐   ☐
c)   743211   ☐   ☐
d)   76599   ☐   ☐
e)   67897   ☐   ☐
f)   74599   ☐   ☐

10.   Highest   Lowest

a)   201198   ☐   ☐

b)   390145   ☐   ☐

c)   301923   ☐   ☐

d)   239061   ☐   ☐

e)   279199   ☐   ☐

f)   391061   ☐   ☐

11.   Highest   Lowest

a)   70654   ☐   ☐

b)   30951   ☐   ☐

c)   40998   ☐   ☐

d)   70897   ☐   ☐

e)   31254   ☐   ☐

f)   70879   ☐   ☐

12.   Highest   Lowest

a)   906786   ☐   ☐

b)   908654   ☐   ☐

c)   906887   ☐   ☐

d)   907654   ☐   ☐

e)   905998   ☐   ☐

f)   901678   ☐   ☐

13.   Highest   Lowest

a)   186546   ☐   ☐

b)   156783   ☐   ☐

c)   176298   ☐   ☐

d)   190867   ☐   ☐

e)   128765   ☐   ☐

f)   138211   ☐   ☐

14.   Highest   Lowest

a)   3598760   ☐   ☐

b)   3789021   ☐   ☐

c)   3276531   ☐   ☐

d)   3789211   ☐   ☐

e)   3675112   ☐   ☐

f)   3542167   ☐   ☐

15.   Highest   Lowest

a)   409678   ☐   ☐

b)   412760   ☐   ☐

c)   400896   ☐   ☐

d)   407206   ☐   ☐

e)   411067   ☐   ☐

f)   402111   ☐   ☐

16.   Highest Lowest

a)   578990   ☐   ☐

b)   576908   ☐   ☐

c)   5786708   ☐   ☐

d)   576819   ☐   ☐

e)   578906   ☐   ☐

f)   579806   ☐   ☐

17.   Highest Lowest

a)   24000960   ☐   ☐

b)   2040066   ☐   ☐

c)   24000866   ☐   ☐

d)   24000009   ☐   ☐

e)   24000899   ☐   ☐

f)   24000006   ☐   ☐

18.   Highest Lowest

a)   81191181   ☐   ☐

b)   82341167   ☐   ☐

c)   82345611   ☐   ☐

d)   81111911   ☐   ☐

e)   81121101   ☐   ☐

f)   82343167   ☐   ☐

19.   Highest Lowest

a)   60765432   ☐   ☐

b)   60845623   ☐   ☐

c)   60946789   ☐   ☐

d)   60498765   ☐   ☐

e)   60467587   ☐   ☐

f)   60476445   ☐   ☐

20.   Highest Lowest

a)   8080978926   ☐   ☐

b)   807986532   ☐   ☐

c)   8078976543   ☐   ☐

d)   8076540009   ☐   ☐

e)   8097650078   ☐   ☐

f)   8097745009   ☐   ☐

21.   Highest Lowest

a)   7876543299   ☐   ☐

b)   7659872496   ☐   ☐

c)   7982534349   ☐   ☐

d)   7980808056   ☐   ☐

e)   7968579909   ☐   ☐

f)   7089898921   ☐   ☐

22.   Highest   Lowest

		Highest	Lowest
a)	4567890643	☐	☐
b)	3567245376	☐	☐
c)	6547821324	☐	☐
d)	6558761289	☐	☐
e)	6559876524	☐	☐
f)	6546789067	☐	☐

23.

		Highest	Lowest
a)	8726354898	☐	☐
b)	8274659098	☐	☐
c)	8634527804	☐	☐
d)	8273097144	☐	☐
e)	8299011274	☐	☐
f)	8634253434	☐	☐

24.

		Highest	Lowest
a)	7689035467	☐	☐
b)	7998724536	☐	☐
c)	7954673826	☐	☐
d)	7645453909	☐	☐
e)	7123498765	☐	☐
f)	79986353423	☐	☐

25.

		Highest	Lowest
a)	6575645387	☐	☐
b)	6578300987	☐	☐
c)	6547835467	☐	☐
d)	6526589990	☐	☐
e)	6547890977	☐	☐
f)	6547843567	☐	☐

26.

		Highest	Lowest
a)	5678905678	☐	☐
b)	5867390765	☐	☐
c)	5876489009	☐	☐
d)	5736999789	☐	☐
e)	5880833567	☐	☐
f)	5880904563	☐	☐

27.

		Highest	Lowest
a)	2134987645	☐	☐
b)	3546216457	☐	☐
c)	1290876356	☐	☐
d)	2314267800	☐	☐
e)	1123789902	☐	☐
f)	21786534	☐	☐

28.   Highest Lowest

a)   4563546455   ☐   ☐

b)   4535473645   ☐   ☐

c)   4545456354   ☐   ☐

d)   4556353435   ☐   ☐

e)   4565534345   ☐   ☐

f)   4534544455   ☐   ☐

29.   Highest Lowest

a)   6794867584   ☐   ☐

b)   6856576874   ☐   ☐

c)   6756575456   ☐   ☐

d)   6756475666   ☐   ☐

e)   6757448765   ☐   ☐

f)   6754567676   ☐   ☐

30.   Highest Lowest

a)   8318475657   ☐   ☐

b)   8237465784   ☐   ☐

c)   8231845675   ☐   ☐

d)   8237465875   ☐   ☐

e)   8231846587   ☐   ☐

f)   8237456897   ☐   ☐

Answers to Test 6

1.	c	d	11.	d	b	21.	c	f
2.	c	e	12.	b	f	22.	e	b
3.	d	f	13.	d	e	23.	a	d
4.	b	a	14.	d	c	24.	b	e
5.	f	e	15.	b	c	25.	b	d
6.	b	d	16.	c	d	26.	f	a
7.	b	d	17.	a	b	27.	b	f
8.	a	e	18.	c	d	28.	e	f
9.	b	e	19.	c	f	29.	b	f
10.	f	a	20.	f	b	30.	a	c

Conversion of scores on Test 6

Test score = number correct minus errors = _____

	Below average				Average		Above average			
Timed score	1	2	3–5	6–9	10–13	14–17	18–21	22–24	25–27	28+
Power score	1	2	3–7	8–12	13–17	18–21	22–24	25–27	28–29	30+
Score out of ten	1	2	3	4	5	6	7	8	9	10

Test 7: Multiple choice

In this book:

+ means add or plus
– means subtract or take away
* or × means multiply or times
/ or ÷ means divide

In this test you have to solve various numerical problems. These are about normal, everyday situations in which numbers are used.

Each problem has four possible answers for you to choose from. You have to decide which answer is correct, then circle or underline your choice. If this is not your book, record your answers on a separate sheet. Also, make sure you have some spare paper for any rough working out you may want to do. Using a calculator is not allowed.

Example 1
What is 6 × 9?

  a) 55.3   b) 5.7   c) 54   d) 567

Example 2
What is ½ of 3?

  a) 1½   b) 1   c) ½   d) 2½

Example 3
What is the sale price of an article if it is reduced 10% from £100?

  a) £99   b) £89   c) £80   d) £90

Answers
The answers are:
   Example 1: c) 54
   Example 2: a) 1½
   Example 3: d) £90.

Make sure you have sufficient spare paper before you start the test. Write your answer in the space provided or on a separate sheet if you should not mark this book.

Timed test: 15 minutes. Power test: 45 minutes.

1. What is 68 + 56 + 107?

    a) 221   b) 231   c) 232   d) 225

2. What is the value of 9 in 967423.0876?

    a) hundreds of thousands   b) hundreds   c) thousands   d) tens

3. 79 × 56

    a) 4,424   b) 4,522   c) 4,363   d) 4,414

4. 5.5 × 0.4

    a) 2.1   b) 2.4   c) 2.2   d) 2.0

5. What is a week's pay at a salary of £24,960 per year?

    a) £500   b) £520   c) £460   d) £480

6. What is the next number in the sequence –8 , 2 , –4 , 4 , 0 , 6 , ?

    a) 8   b) 4   c) –4   d) 0

7. ½ is equal to:

    a) $^{12}/_6$ b) $^2/_1$ c) $^5/_{10}$ d) $^4/_6$

8. $^{29}/_9$ is equal to:

    a) 29 × 9   b) $3^1/_9$ c) 29 ÷ 9   d) 3

9. How much would be a $^1/_5$ deposit on a car costing £18,000?

    a) £1,800   b) £2,400   c) £4,500   d) £3,600

10. What is ½ + ¼ + $^1/_3$?

    a) 1   b) $1^1/_{16}$ c) $1^1/_{12}$ d) $1^1/_9$

11. What is a quarter of £ 680?

    a) £220   b) £170   c) £140   d) £180

12. What fraction must be added to $^2/_7$ + $^2/_5$ to make 1?

    a) $^{24}/_{35}$ b) $^4/_{12}$ c) $^2/_3$ d) $^{11}/_{35}$

13. Which is the same proportion as $\frac{1}{3}$ to $\frac{1}{2}$?

    a) 2 to 3   b) 4 to 5   c) 1 to 3   d) 3 to 4

14. A train travels 360 miles at the rate of 40 miles per hour. Another train travels at 16 miles an hour. What is the distance in miles it will travel in the same time?

    a) 160   b) 144   c) 140   d) 112

15. $\frac{9}{10}$ as a decimal is ...?

    a) 0.09   b) 9   c) 0.9   d) 0.009

16. 3.14 + 4.06 + 7.9

    a) 15.1   b) 15.01   c) 14.1   d) 14.9

17. 1.06 ÷ 0.4

    a) 2.56   b) 0.265   c) 2.65   d) 0.0265

18. What is 0.6 of £500?

    a) £375   b) £340   c) £200   d) £300

19. A ratio of 1½ to 3½ is the same as...?

    a) 2 : 3   b) 5 : 12   c) 8 : 15   d) 14 : 6

20. What is the average of 3.91 , 4.78 , 5.73 and 2.18?

    a) 4.15   b) 4.75   c) 4.25   d) 3.95

21. How long will it take to cover 210 km (kilometres) at an average speed of 120 km/hour?

    a) 2 hours   b) 1 hr 45 min   c) 1½ hours   d) 1 hr 40 min

22. How much will be a tax of 17.5% added to an item costing £80?

    a) £14.50   b) £17.50   c) £15.00   d) £14.00

23. The price of petrol rises from .80 to .90 per litre. What is this as a percentage?

    a) 11%   b) 12.5%   c) 11.25%   d) 10%

24. A ship travelling at 21 knots per hour reaches port in 16 days. How much longer would it take if its speed was 18 knots per hour?

a) $2^1/_3$ days   b) $2^1/_2$ days   c) $2^2/_3$ days   d) $2^1/_9$ days

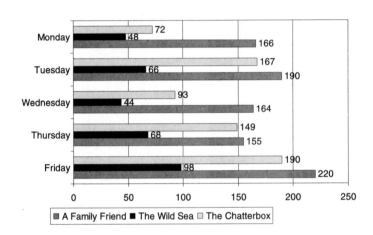

25. The graph shows cinema attendance for three films. What was the week's attendance for 'The Wild Sea'?

a) 314   b) 673   c) 418   d) 324

26. From the graph above, what was the lowest figure for attendance at all three films on any night?

a) 286   b) 301   c) 281   d) 294

27. From the graph above, what was ratio of attendance on Monday of 'The Wild Sea' compared to 'The Chatterbox' as a fraction?

a) $^2/_3$ b) $^3/_5$ c) $^4/_7$ d) $^3/_4$

28. What is the area of the shaded side of the rectangular box below?

a) 30 sq cm   b) 24 sq cm   c) 20 sq cm   d) 30 sq cm

29. What is the total surface area of the rectangular box below?

a) 108 sq cm   b) 100 sq cm   c) 104 sq cm   d) 148 sq cm

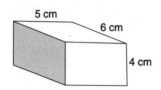

30.   What is the volume of the rectangular box above?

a) 96 cu cm   b) 125 cu cm   c) 120 cu cm   d) 150 cu cm

Answers to Test 7

1. b	11. b	21. b
2. a	12. d	22. d
3. a	13. a	23. b
4. c	14. b	24. c
5. d	15. c	25. d
6. b	16. a	26. a
7. c	17. c	27. a
8. c	18. d	28. b
9. d	19. d	29. d
10. c	20. a	30. c

Conversion of scores on Test 7

Test score = number correct minus errors = _____

	Below average				Average		Above average			
Timed score	1	2	3–4	5–6	7–8	9–10	11–12	13–14	15–17	18+
Power score		1–2	3–5	6–8	9–11	12–15	16–20	21–24	25–27	28+
Score out of ten	1	2	3	4	5	6	7	8	9	10

Relative strength of applied test scores

In the table below circle the score for each of your test results. Join each result with a line to make the relative differences between scores easier to perceive. The greater the difference between tests, the more likely it is that you really are better at one type of test than another. This may be of guidance to you in determining the most suitable area of study, what type of career to pursue or where you may want to enhance your aptitude.

Number usage	1	2	3	4	5	6	7	8	9	10
Proportion	1	2	3	4	5	6	7	8	9	10
Money	1	2	3	4	5	6	7	8	9	10
Graphs and tables	1	2	3	4	5	6	7	8	9	10
Space	1	2	3	4	5	6	7	8	9	10
Accuracy	1	2	3	4	5	6	7	8	9	10
Multiple choice	1	2	3	4	5	6	7	8	9	10

Career guidance

It is difficult to think of anybody who would not require at least some minimum level of numerical aptitude whatever they choose to do in life. The following careers are included because they more obviously require an above average level of numerical aptitude, sometimes well above. It is certainly arguable that there are many other careers that it might have been possible to include.

1. Number
Account executive
Administrator
Airline pilot
Chief executive
Civil servant
Database administrator
Deck officer
Electrical engineer
Electronics engineer
Estate agent
Food scientist
Head teacher
Health services administrator
Helicopter pilot
Lawyer
Managing director
Mathematician
Mathematics teacher
Navigating officer
Physicist
Pilot
Sales executive
Solicitor
Sports centre manager
Systems analyst
Surgeon
Travel agent
Web designer
Web master

2. Proportion
Account planner
Architect
Astronaut
Astronomer
Broker

Buyer
Chef
Design engineer
Designer
Primary school teacher
Engineering officer
Estate manager
Estimator
Geologist
Instrument and control
engineer
Manufacturing manager
Production manager
Publisher
Purchasing manager
Science teacher
Teacher
Theatre administrator
Transport manager
Town Planning officer

3. Money
Accountant
Arts administrator
Auctioneer
Bank manager
Building society manager
Bursar
Cashier
Commercial account manager
Company secretary
Currency trader
Estate manager
Farm manager
Fundraiser
Hotel manager
Human resources manager

Importer/exporter
Insurance agent
Insurance adjuster
Licensee
Merchandiser
Negotiator
Post Office manager
Producer (films)
Property negotiator
Purser
Sales manager
Tax inspector

4. Graphs and tables
Actuary
Business consultant
Civil engineer
Economist
Ergonomist
Financial analyst
Hydrographic surveyor
Information scientist
Investment adviser
Marketing manager
Market researcher
Oceanographer
Securities analyst
Statistician
Stockbroker
Underwriter

5. Space
Accident assessor
Agricultural engineer
Aeronautical engineer
Aeronautical technician
Aircraft engineer

Automobile designer
Boat builder
Building inspector
Building surveyor
Draughtsperson
Engineer
Fashion buyer
Landscape architect
Manufacturing engineer
Mechanical engineer
Mining engineer
Naval architect
Planning technician
Space salesperson
Surveyor

6. Accuracy
Admissions clerk
Aerodrome controller
Auditor
Clerk
Computer technician
Financial controller
Franchise operator
Geneticist
Horologist
Laboratory technician
Legal executive
Merchandiser
Microelectronics engineer
Programmer
Software engineer
Stock controller
Trading Standards officer
Turf accountant
Wages clerk

While the careers have been placed in one of the six categories corresponding with areas of testing, many of them might equally well be placed in another box. Again, many of the careers are hard to classify as they may require aptitude in more than one area or, indeed, all of them. Much depends on where the career takes place and in what circumstances and conditions.

Abstract tests

In Part 3 you will discover your aptitude for numerical reasoning in relation to intelligence testing and in relation to assessment situations, for example, entry to business school and jobs of managerial or senior potential.

Test 8: Deduction

There is a set of nine numbers that relate to each other in a certain way. Find the way the first set of boxes works. The numbers in the second set work in exactly the same way. What number must go in the empty box in the second set of each example? Write your answer in the empty box. If this is not your book, write your answer on a separate sheet of paper.

Example 1

2	1	4
1	2	1
3	3	5

3	1	2
3	2	2
6		4

Example 2

6	1	5
2	1	1
4	2	2

	3	2
7	1	6
8	3	5

Example 3

4	2	6
5	2	8
6	1	11

7	5	
8	8	8
9	10	8

Answers and explanation

In Example 1, the top row of figures is added to the middle row to give the number in the bottom row. Therefore, the answer to Example 1 is 3.

In Example 2, the middle column and the right column are added to give the figures in the left-hand column. Therefore, the answer to Example 2 is 5.

Example 3 is more difficult. The figure in each box on the left-hand column is doubled. Then the figure in the middle column is taken away from it. This gives the figure in each of the boxes in the right-hand column. Thus, starting with the figure in the top-left-hand box, 4 doubled gives 8 and 2 taken away from 8 gives 6. Then 5 doubled gives 10 and 2 taken away from 10 gives 8, and so on. Thus the answer to Example 3 is 9, because 7 doubled is 14 and 5 taken away from 14 gives 9.

In the test the numbers may be arranged in many different ways. Your task is to work out the key to how the numbers relate to each other then use the key to discover the missing number.

Time test: 15 minutes. Power test: 45 minutes.

1.

1	1	1
1	2	3
2	3	4

2	2	2
2	3	4
4	5	

2.

2	3	4
1	2	3
1	1	1

4	5	6
3	4	5
	1	1

3.

1	1	1
5	5	5
7	7	7

2	2	2
3		3
8	8	8

4.

2	1	4
3	2	7
2	2	6

1	1	3
2	3	8
	2	5

5.

11	7	9
6	3	6
5	4	3

	8	6
2	4	5
7	4	1

6.

2	3	5
4	4	7
2	1	2

4	3	7
6		8
2	4	1

7.

2	3	4
1	2	2
2	6	8

3	4	
1	2	2
3	8	6

8.

3	4	3
0	2	2
0	8	6

	5	0
2	1	6
0	5	0

9.

4	2	8
1	1	2
1	0	2

4	8	
2	0	0
0	4	3

10.

2	1	2
1	0	6
0	0	0

3	3	6
1		8
0	0	0

11.

5	2	1
9	3	3
4	2	0

6	2	2
7	3	
8	3	2

12.

4	2	2
4	8	4
0	6	2

5	3	0
6		2
1	5	2

13.

16	14	12
14	12	10
12	10	8

	10	7
10	7	4
7	4	1

14.

6	10	12
2	5	2
3	2	6

14		20
7	2	2
2	8	10

15.

5	6	1
4	6	2
9	9	0

7	8	1
4	7	3
0		4

16.

1	3	5
15	17	7
13	11	9

4	6	8
	20	10
16	14	12

17.

1	2	3
3	18	4
0	4	1

4	2	1
0		1
1	5	1

18.

3	6	1
9	36	1
3	6	1

	5	2
16	25	4
4	5	2

19.

2	0	2
0	9	6
1	0	6

2	2	0
1	1	7
1		3

20.

7	10	13
4	7	10
1	4	7

5	7	9
3		7
1	3	5

21.

5	4	2
3	2	2
8	3	10

4	2	4
6	2	
5	2	6

22.

1	9	3
4	16	2
2	8	2

1	16	4
5	20	2
	2	1

23.

1	1	1
3	4	3
2	3	2

3	2	1
	4	5
2	2	4

24.

3	4	7
7	7	0
4	3	7

4	4	0
7		15
6	4	20

25.

3	6	4
2	5	3
5	11	7

5	7	4
4		8
9	13	12

26.

4	0	4
0	3	2
0	5	2

4	4	2
5	1	6
9	3	

27.

3	2	8
2	1	5
4	3	11

1	4	10
2	2	8
5	3	

28.

2	1	3
3	2	3
7	4	9

1		1
4	1	5
6	7	7

29.

15	12	6
9	3	18
9	3	24

8	6	4
8		18
16	10	24

30.

2	1	9
3	2	25
2	4	36

3	1	16
0	1	
3	4	49

Answers to Test 8

1.	6	11.	1	21.	8
2.	1	12.	8	22.	2
3.	3	13.	13	23.	5
4.	1	14.	16	24.	8
5.	9	15.	4	25.	6
6.	7	16.	18	26.	4
7.	3	17.	15	27.	12
8.	0	18.	4	28.	3
9.	6	19.	0	29.	2
10.	6	20.	5	30.	0

Conversion of scores on Test 8

	Below average				Average		Above average			
Timed score	1	2	3	4	5–7	8–11	12–14	15–19	20–23	24+
Power score		1–3	4–6	7–9	10–13	14–17	18–21	22–24	25–26	27+
Score out of ten	1	2	3	4	5	6	7	8	9	10

Test 9: Concept formation

In this test you have to work out the pattern (or rule or formula) that is provided from two sets of figures in boxes. From this you have to work out what figures go into the third set of boxes.

You are given three sets of numbers that go together in a certain way. In the third set there are two question marks (?) that show where numbers are missing. From the alternatives provided, you have to choose the set that would complete the third set properly.

Underline or tick the correct answer. If this is not your book, write your answers on a separate sheet of paper.

Example 1

a)

b)

c)

d)

e)

f)

Example 2

Example 3

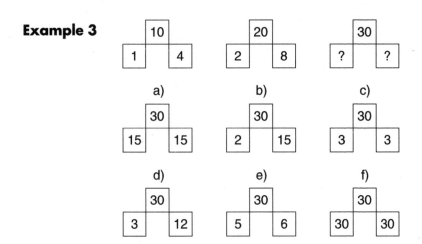

Answers and explanation

In Example 1, the figures are all 1s, then all 2s and then all 3s. The answer is f).

In Example 2, the figure in the bottom right-hand square of each group of three boxes is the sum of the other two boxes. So, 2 + 2 = 4, then 3 + 2 = 5. Another way to find the answer is to subtract the bottom left box from the bottom right box to give the top box. From the alternatives provided only answer c) follows a correct rule, as 4 + 4 = 8 or 8 – 4 = 4. None of the other alternatives follow the same pattern or formula as the first and second set of boxes.

In Example 3, the rule is to add the two bottom boxes in each set and then double this number to give the figure in the top box. Thus, $1 + 4 = 5 \times 2 = 10$, $2 + 8 = 10 \times 2 = 20$. The answer is d), as $3 + 12 = 15 \times 2 = 30$. None of the other alternatives follow the correct rule or formula to produce the number 30.

Each item in the test is a separate problem and therefore follows a different formula. Your task is to find how the numbers relate to each other and choose the most logical answer from those provided.

Timed test: 15 minutes. Power test 45 minutes.

1.

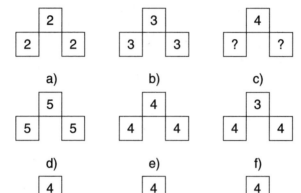

2.

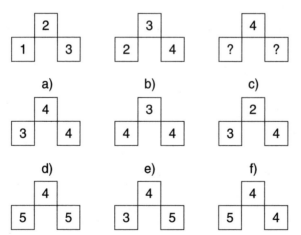

3.

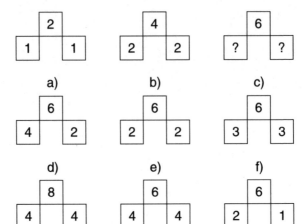

4.

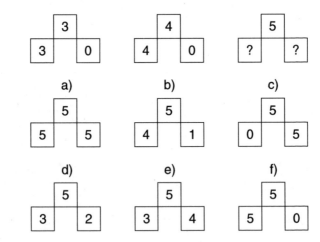

5.

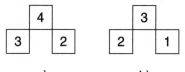

```
    a)              b)              c)
   ___             ___             ___
  | 2 |           | 2 |           | 2 |
 _|   |_         _|   |_         _|   |_
| 1 | 0 |       | 1 | 1 |       | 0 | 0 |
|___|___|       |___|___|       |___|___|

    d)              e)              f)
   ___             ___             ___
  | 2 |           | 2 |           | 2 |
 _|   |_         _|   |_         _|   |_
| 2 | 2 |       | 0 | 1 |       | 1 | 3 |
|___|___|       |___|___|       |___|___|
```

6.

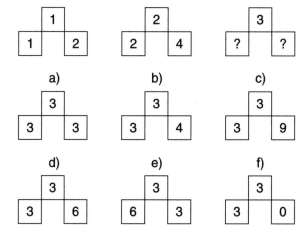

7.

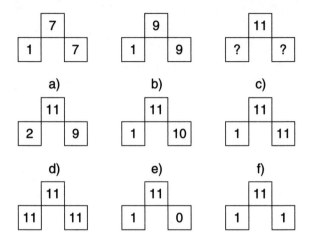

8.

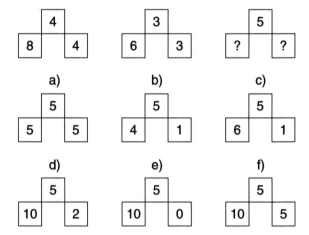

9.

10.

11.

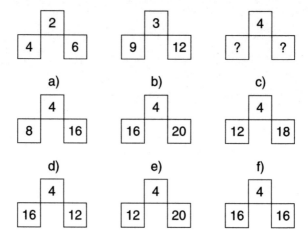

12.

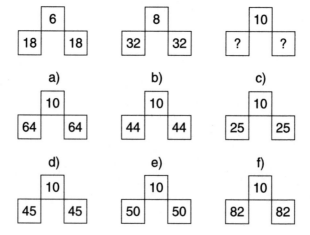

13.

| | 2 | |
| 3 | | 10 |

| | 4 | |
| 2 | | 12 |

| | 6 | |
| ? | | ? |

a)

| | 6 | |
| 0 | | 14 |

b)

| | 6 | |
| 2 | | 12 |

c)

| | 6 | |
| 1 | | 14 |

d)

| | 6 | |
| 3 | | 14 |

e)

| | 6 | |
| 4 | | 10 |

f)

| | 6 | |
| 4 | | 14 |

14.

| | 3 | |
| 4 | | 5 |

| | 5 | |
| 19 | | 6 |

| | 7 | |
| ? | | ? |

a)

| | 7 | |
| 25 | | 7 |

b)

| | 7 | |
| 36 | | 7 |

c)

| | 7 | |
| 41 | | 7 |

d)

| | 7 | |
| 14 | | 7 |

e)

| | 7 | |
| 49 | | 7 |

f)

| | 7 | |
| 40 | | 9 |

15.

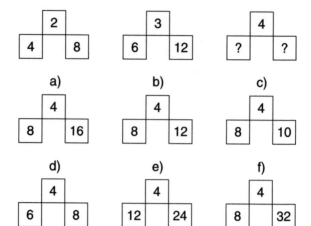

16.

17.

14		20		34	
1	6	2	8	?	?

a)		b)		c)	
34		34		34	
12	21	5	12	4	16

d)		e)		f)	
34		34		34	
4	9	7	9	2	17

18.

12		6		8	
9	3	4	7	?	?

a)		b)		c)	
8		8		8	
5	3	5	7	3	5

d)		e)		f)	
8		8		8	
5	9	3	9	5	6

19.

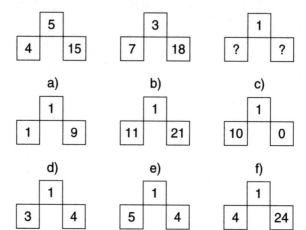

20.

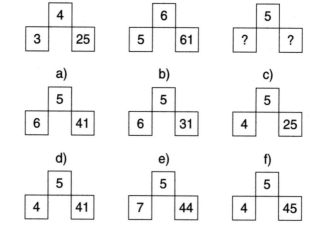

21.

a)

b)

c)

d)

e)

f)

22.

a)

b)

c)

d)

e)

f)

23.

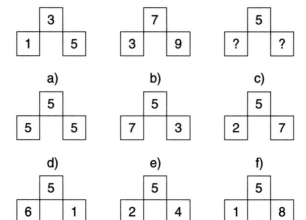

24.

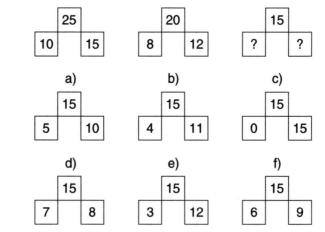

25.

a) b) c)

d) e) f)

26.

a) b) c)

d) e) f)

27.

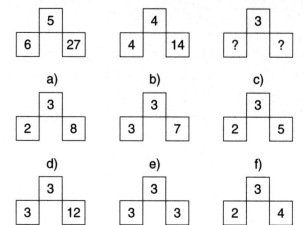

28.

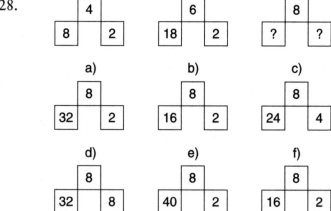

29.

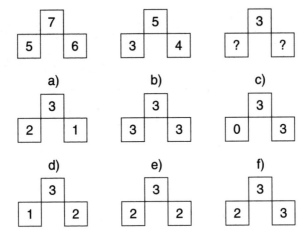

30.

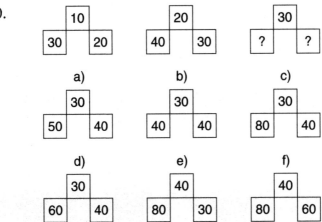

Answers to Test 9

1.	b	11.	b	21.	c
2.	e	12.	e	22.	a
3.	c	13.	c	23.	c
4.	f	14.	f	24.	f
5.	a	15.	a	25.	a
6.	d	16.	e	26.	e
7.	c	17.	b	27.	c
8.	f	18.	d	28.	a
9.	d	19.	e	29.	d
10.	a	20.	d	30.	a

Conversion of scores on Test 9

	Below average				Average		Above average			
Timed score	1	2	3–4	5–7	8–10	11–13	14–18	19–22	23–27	28+
Power score		1–3	4–7	8–11	12–15	16–18	19–22	23–25	26–27	28+
Score out of ten	1	2	3	4	5	6	7	8	9	10

Test 10: Sequential logic

You are given a set of numbers that go together in a certain way. One number is missing. The place where the missing number should be is given by the question mark (?). From the alternatives provided, you have to choose the number that would go in the place of the question mark in order to complete the set properly.

Underline or tick the correct answer. If this is not your book, mark your answers on a separate sheet of paper.

Example 1

| 2 | 4 | ? | 8 | 10 | 12 |

a) 3   b) 5   c) 7   d) 6   e) 4

Example 2

| 7 ½ | 6 | 4 ½ | 3 | 1 ½ | ? |

a) ½   b) 1   c) 0   d) –1 ½   e) 3

Example 3

| 2 | 6 | 15 | 31 | ? | 92 |

a) 42   b) 56   c) 46   d) 51   e) 61

Answers and explanation

In Example 1, the numbers are increased by two each time. The missing number is 6, so the answer is d).

In Example 2, the series is reducing by one and a half each time. The answer is c).

Example 3 is more difficult and is a type that you will find much later in the real test. This series is worked when you have discovered that the square of 2, then 3, then 4, then 5, then 6 is added to each of the numbers in the series.

To explain: the square of 2, which is 4 (that is, 2 × 2 = 4) has been added to the first number to give 6.

Then the square of 3, which is 9 (that is, 3 × 3 = 9) has been added to 6 to give 15.

Then the square of 4, which is 16, has been added to 15 to give 31.

Then the square of 5, which is 25, can be added to 31 to give 56.

Finally, if the square of 6, which is 36 is added to 56 it gives 92. This completes the series properly. The answer is therefore b).

Each of the series in the test is a separate problem and therefore follows different rules. Your task to find how the series is connected and choose the most logical answer from those provided.

Timed test: 10 minutes. Power test: 30 minutes.

1.   1   3   5   ?   9   11   13
      a) 9   b) 2   c) 10 d) 7   e) 8

2.   12   ?   8   6   4   2
      a) 10 b) 0   c) 11 d) 9   e) 8

3.   100   90   80   70   ?   50
      a) 55 b) 0   c) 40 d) 50 e) 60

4.   5   6   8   11   15   ?
      a) 17 b) 20 c) 18 d) 16 e) 21

5.   ?   2   5   10   17   26
      a) 2   b) 5   c) 1   d) 0   e) ½

6. 0   1   1   2   3   ?
    a) 2   b) 4   c) 5   d) 6   e) 3

7. 0.6   1.2   ?   2.4   3.0   3.6
    a) 1.4 b) 1.6 c) 2.0 d) 1.8 e) 2.2

8. ?   97   93   85   69   37
    a) 94   b) 101 c) 100 d) 103 e) 99

9. 1   ?   7   10   13   16
    a) 3   b) 4   c) 2   d) 5   e) 1

10. 102   91   80   ?   58   47
    a) 69   b) 71   c) 65   d) 70   e) 66

11. 3   2   4   3   5   ?
    a) 4   b) 5   c) 3   d) 6   e) 8

12. 0.1   1.0   1.1   11.0   ?   111.0
    a) 11.00   b) 12.0   c) 10.1   d) 11.1   e) 100.0

13. 13   ?   12   13   11   12
    a) 13   b) 14   c) 12   d) 15   e) 11

14. 1   2   4   ?   16   32
    a) 6   b) 10   c) 8   d) 9   e) 5

15. 0   9   9   18   27   ?
    a) 27   b) 36   c) 54   d) 45   e) 9

16. 3   ?   9   15   24   39
    a) 3   b) 0   c) 9   d) 12   e) 6

17.   ?   1.25   1.0   1.5   1.25   1.75
       a) 0.75   b) 1.0   c) 0.5   d) 0.25   e) 0.125

18.   3   6   5   8   7   ?
       a) 9   b) 11   c) 7   d) 15   e) 10

19.   1   2   3   6   12   ?
       a) 48   b) 24   c) 16   d) 22   e) 18

20.   48   39   ?   24   18   13
       a) 31   b) 30   c) 29   d) 32   e) 33

21   ?   25   20   20   10   15
      a) 30   b) 25   c) 20   d) 5   e) 35

22.   4   9   20   43   ?   185
       a) 92   b) 65   c) 63   d) 90   e) 96

23.   5   6   8   12   20   ?
       a) 30   b) 32   c) 36   d) 34   e) 48

24.   2   2   3   5   8   ?
       a) 12   b) 10   c) 8   d) 13   e) 11

25.   17   ?   34   26   68   52
       a) 21   b) 26   c) 8   d) 17   e) 13

26.   ?   11   23   45   91   181
       a) 5   b) 7   c) 12   d) 6   e) 9

27.   1   3   3   9   ?   243
       a) 12   b) 27   c) 54   d) 72   e) 81

28.   364   ?   8   22   14   170

     a) 113 b) 34 c) 7 d) 85 e) 5

29.   17   14   31   ?   76   121

     a) 62 b) 46 c) 45 d) 48 e) 114

30.   43   31   21   13   7   ?

     a) 3 b) 4 c) 7 d) 5 e) 6

Answers to Test 10

1. d	11. a	21. a
2. a	12. d	22. d
3. e	13. b	23. c
4. b	14. c	24. a
5. c	15. d	25. e
6. c	16. e	26. d
7. d	17. a	27. b
8. e	18. e	28. b
9. b	19. b	29. c
10. a	20. a	30. a

Conversion of scores on Test 10

	Below average				Average		Above average			
Timed score	1	2	3–4	5–6	7–8	9–11	12–14	15–19	20–24	25+
Power score	1	2–4	5–9	10–13	14–16	17–19	20–23	24–26	27–28	29+
Score out of ten	1	2	3	4	5	6	7	8	9	10

Test 11: Construct analysis

In this test the top box has a relationship with the box below it. The boxes on the left-hand side have the same relationship to the boxes on the right-hand side. From working out what happens in the boxes on the left-hand side, work out the figures that should go in the empty boxes on the right-hand side. Choose from the alternatives provided.

Example 1

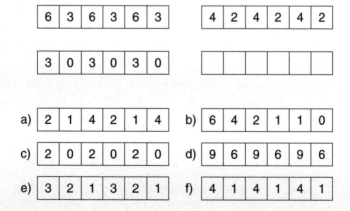

Example 3

4	3	2	2	6	0

9	7	6	3	2	1

0	6	2	2	3	4

a)
2	4	3	5	6	0

b)
4	3	0	6	2	2

c)
0	3	6	7	9	7

d)
3	0	9	8	7	6

e)
3	4	3	0	1	0

f)
1	2	3	6	7	9

Answers and explanation

In Example 1, there is a regular pattern of 4s. Underneath, there is a regular pattern of 2s, which are half each of the 4s. On the right there is a regular pattern of 6s. From the alternatives provided, there is a regular pattern of 3s, which are half the 6s above. This follows the same rule as the 4s and the 2s. None of the other alternatives have a logical relationship. Therefore the answer is e).

In Example 2, the rule for the empty set of boxes is to take away the second number from the first number. Thus, take 3 from 6 in the top left-hand box and then 3 from 3 in the box underneath. Then, in the top right-hand box, 2 is taken from 4 in each case. The only answer that 'fits' is answer c) because 2 is taken away in each case. Also, the lower figure of 3 in the top left-hand set begins the bottom set, while the lower figure of 2 in the top right-hand set begins the bottom set, which also 'fits'. None of the other alternatives have a logical relationship.

In Example 3, the numbers in the bottom sets are the reverse of those in the top sets. None of the other alternatives have a logical relationship. The answer is therefore f).

Each item in the test is a separate problem and therefore follows a different rule. Your task is to find how the numbers relate to each other and choose the most logical and fitting answer from those provided. If this is not your book, write your answers on a separate sheet of paper.

Timed test: 15 minutes. Power test: 45 minutes.

1.

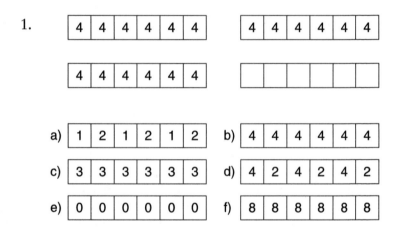

2.

1	2	3	4	5	6

2	3	4	5	6	7

1	2	3	4	5	6

a)
1	2	3	4	5	6

b)
6	5	4	3	2	1

c)
2	3	4	5	6	7

d)
2	4	6	8	10	12

e)
3	6	5	4	2	1

f)
7	8	9	10	11	12

3.

1	2	1	2	1	2

3	4	3	4	3	4

2	1	2	1	2	1

a)
1	1	1	1	1	1

b)
2	2	2	2	2	2

c)
4	4	4	3	3	3

d)
4	3	4	3	4	3

e)
3	4	4	4	4	3

f)
3	3	3	4	4	4

4.

2	0	0	0	0	4

4	0	0	0	0	6

1	0	0	0	0	2

a)
5	0	0	0	0	5

b)
2	0	0	0	0	3

c)
3	0	0	0	0	3

d)
1	0	0	0	0	3

e)
2	0	0	0	0	5

f)
6	0	0	0	0	3

5.

6	5	4	3	2	1

1	2	3	4	5	6

1	2	3	4	5	6

a)
4	5	6	1	2	3

b)
1	2	3	6	5	4

c)
6	5	4	3	2	1

d)
6	5	4	1	2	3

e)
5	6	1	2	3	4

f)
3	2	1	3	2	1

6.

5	0	4	0	3	0

6	0	5	0	4	0

0	4	0	3	0	2

a)
0	5	5	0	4	4

b)
0	4	0	5	0	6

c)
0	5	0	6	0	7

d)
0	7	0	6	0	5

e)
7	0	6	0	5	0

f)
0	5	0	4	0	3

7.

1	1	1	1	1	1

2	2	2	2	2	2

3	3	3	3	3	3

a)
5	5	5	5	5	5

b)
4	4	4	4	4	4

c)
0	0	0	0	0	0

d)
7	7	7	7	7	7

e)
6	6	6	6	6	6

f)
5	5	5	6	6	6

8.

| 2 | 1 | 3 | 1 | 4 | 1 |

| 4 | 3 | 5 | 3 | 6 | 3 |

| 3 | 2 | 4 | 2 | 5 | 2 |

| | | | | | |

a)

| 5 | 4 | 6 | 4 | 7 | 4 |

b)

| 5 | 3 | 5 | 3 | 5 | 3 |

c)

| 4 | 2 | 4 | 2 | 4 | 2 |

d)

| 5 | 4 | 5 | 4 | 5 | 4 |

e)

| 6 | 5 | 5 | 7 | 5 | 8 |

f)

| 6 | 3 | 7 | 3 | 8 | 3 |

9.

| 1 | 3 | 2 | 4 | 1 | 3 |

| 3 | 1 | 2 | 2 | 1 | 3 |

| 2 | 6 | 4 | 8 | 2 | 6 |

| | | | | | |

a)

| 2 | 6 | 4 | 8 | 2 | 6 |

b)

| 1 | 3 | 2 | 4 | 1 | 3 |

c)

| 3 | 1 | 2 | 2 | 1 | 3 |

d)

| 4 | 5 | 3 | 2 | 1 | 3 |

e)

| 6 | 2 | 4 | 4 | 2 | 6 |

f)

| 6 | 2 | 4 | 3 | 2 | 3 |

10.

2	1	3	4	4	1

3	2	1	3	2	1

2	1	3	4	4	2

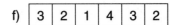

a)
3	2	1	3	2	2

b)
6	4	2	6	4	2

c)
2	1	3	4	4	2

d)
1	2	3	1	2	3

e)
1	4	4	3	2	1

f)
3	2	1	4	3	2

11.

3	0	3	3	0	3

4	0	4	4	0	4

6	3	6	6	3	6

a)
6	0	6	6	0	6

b)
8	0	8	8	0	8

c)
4	4	4	4	4	4

d)
4	8	4	4	8	4

e)
8	0	4	4	0	8

f)
8	4	8	8	4	8

12.

| 1 | 2 | 3 | 3 | 2 | 1 |

| 4 | 3 | 2 | 2 | 3 | 4 |

| 3 | 2 | 1 | 1 | 2 | 3 |

| | | | | | |

a) | 4 | 2 | 3 | 4 | 2 | 3 | b) | 2 | 3 | 4 | 4 | 3 | 2 |

c) | 4 | 2 | 3 | 3 | 2 | 4 | d) | 8 | 6 | 4 | 4 | 6 | 8 |

e) | 3 | 2 | 4 | 3 | 2 | 4 | f) | 2 | 2 | 3 | 3 | 4 | 4 |

13.

| 2 | 2 | 4 | 4 | 4 | 8 |

| 4 | 4 | 6 | 6 | 6 | 10 |

| 1 | 1 | 2 | 2 | 2 | 4 |

| | | | | | |

a) | 4 | 4 | 8 | 4 | 4 | 8 | b) | 3 | 3 | 6 | 6 | 6 | 10 |

c) | 2 | 2 | 3 | 3 | 3 | 8 | d) | 3 | 3 | 6 | 3 | 3 | 6 |

e) | 2 | 2 | 3 | 3 | 3 | 5 | f) | 2 | 2 | 3 | 3 | 3 | 6 |

14.

2	1	1	3	1	5

2	3	1	1	1	8

3	1	1	4	1	6

a)

3	4	1	1	1	9

b)

1	1	1	1	1	7

c)

2	1	3	1	1	4

d)

1	2	1	2	1	2

e)

3	1	1	1	1	9

f)

4	6	1	2	1	9

15.

7	1	6	1	5	1

12	3	9	3	6	3

14	2	12	2	10	2

a)

24	3	21	3	18	3

b)

36	6	30	6	24	6

c)

36	12	24	12	12	0

d)

36	9	27	9	18	9

e)

18	6	12	6	6	0

f)

18	3	15	3	12	3

16.

2	1	0	1	3	4

1	2	3	5	4	0

2	2	0	2	3	4

a)
2	4	6	10	8	0

b)
2	2	3	5	4	1

c)
1	4	3	5	4	0

d)
2	2	6	5	2	2

e)
2	2	3	5	4	0

f)
3	2	1	0	5	4

17.

3	1	2	6	2	4

2	3	3	4	6	8

4	2	3	8	4	6

a)
4	6	8	2	3	3

b)
3	4	4	6	8	10

c)
3	4	4	6	8	8

d)
4	6	6	6	9	9

e)
5	6	6	6	8	4

f)
3	4	5	6	7	9

18.

| 2 | 4 | 6 | 8 | 10 | 12 |

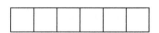

| 3 | 6 | 9 | 12 | 15 | 18 |

| | | | | | |

a) | 16 | 18 | 20 | 22 | 24 | 26 |

b) | 2 | 3 | 4 | 5 | 6 | 7 |

c) | 4 | 10 | 12 | 14 | 16 | 18 |

d) | 6 | 9 | 12 | 15 | 18 | 21 |

e) | 5 | 10 | 15 | 20 | 25 | 30 |

f) | 8 | 12 | 16 | 20 | 24 | 28 |

19.

| 2 | 1 | 2 | 2 | 1 | 2 |

| 3 | 2 | 3 | 3 | 2 | 3 |

| 1 | 2 | 1 | 1 | 2 | 1 |

| | | | | | |

a) | 3 | 3 | 2 | 2 | 3 | 3 |

b) | 2 | 3 | 3 | 3 | 3 | 2 |

c) | 2 | 3 | 2 | 2 | 3 | 2 |

d) | 2 | 3 | 2 | 3 | 3 | 2 |

e) | 2 | 1 | 2 | 2 | 1 | 2 |

f) | 3 | 1 | 2 | 2 | 1 | 3 |

20.

0	1	2	3	4	5

4	5	0	1	2	3

5	0	1	2	3	4

a)
5	4	3	2	1	0

b)
0	1	2	3	4	5

c)
3	4	5	0	1	2

d)
2	3	4	5	0	1

e)
1	2	3	4	5	0

f)
4	5	1	2	3	0

21.

1	2	3	9	4	1

1	6	5	2	2	1

2	3	1	1	9	4

a)
6	5	1	1	2	2

b)
5	6	1	2	1	2

c)
6	1	6	1	2	2

d)
1	1	6	5	2	2

e)
2	6	5	4	4	1

f)
6	1	5	2	1	2

22.

5	1	6	1	1	2

4	0	5	2	2	1

12	0	0	0	0	4

a)
8	0	0	4	0	0

b)
9	0	0	0	0	5

c)
2	0	1	1	0	2

d)
4	0	0	0	2	0

e)
15	5	2	2	0	6

f)
11	0	0	0	4	4

23.

7	0	0	0	0	6

5	0	0	0	0	8

3	5	0	0	0	3

a)
8	0	0	0	0	5

b)
3	5	0	0	0	4

c)
2	5	0	0	0	4

d)
8	0	5	0	0	4

e)
5	8	0	0	0	4

f)
0	4	0	5	0	2

24.

1	3	2	4	3	2

2	3	1	4	3	2

3	7	5	9	7	5

a)

2	3	4	1	3	2

b)

5	4	3	7	6	5

c)

1	3	2	4	3	2

d)

4	6	2	8	6	4

e)

5	6	3	3	6	5

f)

5	7	3	9	7	5

25.

2	1	3	4	5	0

2	3	4	0	1	5

0	0	1	5	0	0

a)

0	0	1	5	0	0

b)

0	0	3	1	0	0

c)

0	1	0	3	0	1

d)

5	1	0	4	3	2

e)

1	0	0	0	0	5

f)

0	5	0	0	1	0

26.

| 2 | 0 | 3 | 0 | 4 | 0 |

| 0 | 3 | 0 | 4 | 0 | 5 |

| 0 | 2 | 0 | 3 | 0 | 4 |

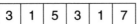

a)

| 0 | 1 | 0 | 2 | 0 | 3 |

b)

| 3 | 0 | 4 | 0 | 5 | 0 |

c)

| 0 | 4 | 0 | 5 | 0 | 6 |

d)

| 2 | 0 | 3 | 0 | 4 | 0 |

e)

| 4 | 0 | 5 | 0 | 6 | 0 |

f)

| 1 | 0 | 2 | 0 | 3 | 0 |

27.

| 3 | 1 | 5 | 3 | 1 | 7 |

| 5 | 3 | 1 | 7 | 5 | 1 |

| 1 | 3 | 7 | 3 | 1 | 5 |

a)

| 3 | 1 | 7 | 5 | 5 | 1 |

b)

| 7 | 5 | 1 | 1 | 3 | 7 |

c)

| 6 | 5 | 3 | 1 | 7 | 4 |

d)

| 1 | 5 | 7 | 3 | 1 | 5 |

e)

| 4 | 2 | 4 | 6 | 4 | 2 |

f)

| 5 | 7 | 1 | 5 | 3 | 1 |

28.

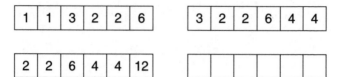

| 1 | 1 | 3 | 2 | 2 | 6 |

| 3 | 2 | 2 | 6 | 4 | 4 |

| 2 | 2 | 6 | 4 | 4 | 12 |

| | | | | | |

a)

| 4 | 4 | 6 | 4 | 4 | 6 |

b)

| 2 | 3 | 2 | 4 | 6 | 6 |

c)

| 6 | 4 | 4 | 12 | 4 | 8 |

d)

| 6 | 4 | 4 | 4 | 4 | 6 |

e)

| 6 | 4 | 4 | 12 | 8 | 8 |

f)

| 6 | 4 | 8 | 12 | 4 | 8 |

29.

| 4 | 1 | 3 | 4 | 0 | 2 |

| 3 | 2 | 0 | 4 | 1 | 2 |

| 0 | 4 | 4 | 3 | 2 | 1 |

| | | | | | |

a)

| 6 | 4 | 0 | 8 | 2 | 4 |

b)

| 3 | 2 | 4 | 1 | 2 | 0 |

c)

| 6 | 3 | 1 | 8 | 2 | 3 |

d)

| 4 | 2 | 8 | 6 | 4 | 0 |

e)

| 0 | 4 | 6 | 8 | 2 | 4 |

f)

| 4 | 0 | 2 | 1 | 0 | 3 |

30.

| 1 | 4 | 2 | 5 | 3 | 6 |

| 2 | 5 | 3 | 6 | 4 | 7 |

| 6 | 1 | 3 | 4 | 5 | 2 |

| | | | | | |

a)

| 5 | 3 | 6 | 2 | 4 | 7 |

b)

| 7 | 4 | 6 | 3 | 5 | 2 |

c)

| 7 | 2 | 4 | 5 | 6 | 3 |

d)

| 7 | 4 | 3 | 6 | 2 | 5 |

e)

| 3 | 6 | 5 | 4 | 2 | 7 |

f)

| 7 | 5 | 4 | 2 | 6 | 3 |

Answers to Test 11

1. b
2. c
3. d
4. b
5. c
6. f
7. e
8. a
9. b or e
10. a

11. f
12. b
13. e
14. a
15. d
16. e
17. b
18. e
19. c
20. c

21. a
22. b
23. c
24. f
25. a
26. b
27. f
28. e
29. b
30. c

Conversion of scores on Test 11

		Below average			Average			Above average		
Timed score			1	2–4	5–7	7–10	11–14	15–18	19–22	23+
Power score		1–2	3–5	6–8	9–11	12–15	16–19	20–23	24–27	28+
Score out of ten	1	2	3	4	5	6	7	8	9	10

Test 12: Power synthesis

In this test you are given a string of numbers. Some of the numbers are in a white circle and some are on a circle with a dark background. You have to work out which **two** numbers go next at the end of the string. You also have to work out whether the numbers are in a white or dark circle.

All the possible answers are provided for you in the chart. Each possible answer has a letter next to it. You have to find the correct number and letter in the chart and then write the letter in the space provided.

It is the letter next to the correct number that is wanted as your answer. Write the letter in the space. If this is not your book, write your answer on a separate sheet of paper. Remember, both letters are necessary to obtain a correct answer. Example 1 has been done for you.

Possible answers

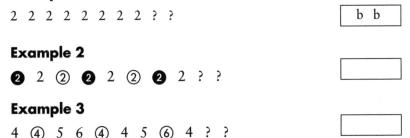

Example 1

2 2 2 2 2 2 2 2 ? ?

b b

Example 2

❷ 2 ② ❷ 2 ② ❷ 2 ? ?

Example 3

4 ④ 5 6 ④ 4 5 ⑥ 4 ? ?

Answers and explanation

In Example 1 the string is a series of the number 2. The next in the string will be a 2 and then a 2 again. In the chart the letter b goes with the number 2 and therefore a 'b' and a 'b' is the correct answer.

In Example 2 the string is again a series of the number 2, but there is also a sequence of circles. This sequence is a white and a dark circle, a plain number, then the white and dark circle. The pattern repeats itself. The next in the string would therefore be a 2 in a white circle and a 2 in a dark circle. The letters that go with these numbers in the chart are 'h' and 'n'. You have to get both letters to have a correct answer.

In Example 3 the sequence of numbers is 4 4 5 6. Every third number is in a white circle. The answer is 'd' and 'k'.

Remember, you must be accurate with both letters to get the correct answer.

Possible answers

a1	b2	c3	d4	e5	f6
g①	h②	i③	j④	k⑤	l⑥
m❶	n❷	o❸	p❹	q❺	r❻

Timed test: 15 minutes. Power test: 45 minutes.

1. 3 3 3 3 3 3 3 ? ?

2. 3 ③ 3 ③ 3 ③ 3 ③ ? ?

3. 4 ❶ 4 ❶ 4 ❶ 4 ① ? ?

4. ❻ 1 ❸ ❻ 1 ❸ ❻ 1 ❸ ? ?

5. ② 1 1 ② 1 1 ② 1 1 ② ? ?

6. ❺ 2 ❻ 5 ❷ 6 ❺ 2 ❻ 5 ? ?

7. ④ 1 3 4 ① 3 4 1 ③ 4 ? ?

8. ❸ 3 5 ❸ 3 5 ❸ 3 5 ❸ ? ?

9. 2 ⑥ 2 ❷ 6 ② 2 ❻ 2 ② ? ?

10. 5 ① ③ ❸ 5 ① ③ ❸ 5 ① ③ ? ?

11. 2 ⑥ 1 2 ⑥ 1 2 ⑥ 1 2 ? ?

12. ③ 4 ❹ ① 3 4 ④ 1 ❸ ? ?

13. 2 ① 3 4 ② 1 3 ④ 2 1 ③ ? ?

14. ③ ❸ ❹ 2 ③ ❸ ❹ 2 ③ ? ?

Possible answers

a1	b2	c3	d4	e5	f6
g①	h②	i③	j④	k⑤	l⑥
m❶	n❷	o❸	p❹	q❺	r❻

15. 1 ⑤ 1 2 ① 5 1 ② 1 5 ? ?

16. 6 ⑥ 3 ❹ 6 ⑥ 3 ❹ 6 ⑥ 3 ? ?

17. 2 3 ① 2 1 ② 3 1 ② 1 2 ③ ? ?

18. ❹ 5 6 2 ③ 4 5 6 ❷ 3 4 5 ? ?

19. 4 ② 1 6 ⑥ 4 2 ① 6 6 ④ 2 ? ?

20. ❸ 1 ❸ ④ ❺ 3 ❶ ③ ❹ 5 ❸ ① ❸ ? ?

21. ⑥ ❶ 6 1 ③ 6 1 6 ① ❸ 6 1 ⑥ ❶ ? ?

22. ④ 6 ② 5 ❸ ④ 6 ② 5 ❸ ④ 6 ② ? ?

23. 2 ① 1 ❺ ❹ 3 ② 1 ① 5 ❹ ❸ 2 ① 1 ? ?

24. 4 ③ ⑤ 1 2 ❹ ❸ 5 1 ② ④ 3 5 ❶ ❷ ? ?

25. ❶ 1 ❷ 5 3 ⑥ ❶ 1 ❷ 5 3 ⑥ ❶ 1 ❷ 5 ? ?

Possible answers

a1	b2	c3	d4	e5	f6
g①	h②	i③	j④	k⑤	l⑥
m❶	n❷	o❸	p❹	q❺	r❻

26. ④ ❸ 6 3 ④ ⑥ ❹ 3 6 ③
④ ❻ 4 3 ⑥ ? ?

27. ① 2 3 ② ❺ 2 1 ② 3 2 ⑤
❷ 1 2 ③ 2 ? ?

28. ④ 3 2 ① ❻ ⑤ 4 3 ② ❶
⑥ 5 4 ③ ? ?

29   6 ❶ ❹ 3 1 4 ⑥ ① 4 3 1
❹ ❻ 1 4 3 ? ?

30. 2 ① ③ 1 5 ⑥ 2 ❶ ❸ 1 5
❻ 2 ① ③ 1 ? ?

Answers to Test 12

1.	c	c	11.	l	a	21.	c	f
2.	c	i	12.	j	d	22.	e	o
3.	d	m	13.	d	b	23.	k	d
4.	r	a	14.	o	p	24.	d	c
5.	a	a	15.	g	b	25.	c	l
6.	n	f	16.	p	f	26.	i	p
7.	a	c	17.	a	b	27.	e	h
8.	c	e	18.	l	b	28.	n	g
9.	f	n	19.	a	l	29.	g	j
10.	o	e	20.	d	q	30.	e	l

Conversion of scores on Test 12

	Below average				Average		Above average			
Timed score	1	2	3	4–5	6–8	9–10	11–13	14–16	17–20	21+
Power score	1	2	3–5	6–8	9–12	13–16	17–20	21–24	25–27	28+
Score out of ten	1	2	3	4	5	6	7	8	9	10

Relative strength of abstract test scores

In the table below, circle the score for each of your test results. Join each result with a line to make the relative differences between scores easier to perceive.

Deduction	1	2	3	4	5	6	7	8	9	10
Concept formation	1	2	3	4	5	6	7	8	9	10
Sequential logic	1	2	3	4	5	6	7	8	9	10
Construct analysis	1	2	3	4	5	6	7	8	9	10
Power synthesis	1	2	3	4	5	6	7	8	9	10

The greater the difference between tests, the more likely it is that you really are better at one type of test than another. This may be of guidance to you in determining the most suitable area of study, what type of career to pursue or where you may want to enhance your aptitude.

Comparison between applied and abstract tests

Compare your results on the abstract tests with those you obtained on the applied tests. If your scores on the abstract tests are generally higher this will indicate that your attainments in areas of working with numbers have not yet reached your potential. This is the very reason that abstract tests are given: to try to establish where there may be scope for development or training. It is the reason why people who score high on abstract tests may be given a job or training or a place on a course in preference to other people who may well appear, because of the qualifications they already possess, to be better candidates; it is because high scores on abstract tests suggest that a person may be able to go as far or even further than the level indicated by a conventional exam result.

On the other hand, when the scores on the practical tests are generally higher than scores on the abstract tests, there are concrete indications of reliable performance that can be matched usefully against definite areas of work. Whereas the abstract scores may suggest promise, the practical scores have a much more certain prediction than can be applied more readily. It is because the practical tests have a more obvious application that they can suggest areas of work in which talent on the tests can be effective in useful ways that are immediately comprehensible.

This is not so with the abstract tests, which are much more concerned with the long-term development or with higher level positions of employment. You will find them used as intelligence tests as part of the selection process from secondary school age up to university entrance. You will find them commonly used by business schools and also by many organizations in the public as well as the private sectors. Here, they are frequently given as part of management selection or assessment programmes or as part of the recruitment of senior managers in whom higher level and broad reasoning abilities are a form of security as they suggest that a candidate will be able to confront multiple, complex tasks.

Career guidance

Your abstract numerical aptitude can be of relevance in many careers and it is difficult to tease apart the discrete talents sought after by the separate tests. In other words, the same job or task at work may be equally well performed by two people whose approach to problem solving may be different, for example one may be logical while the other is intuitive. However, here are some suggestions as to where your potential may be considered especially valuable.

Deduction
Accident assessor
Administrator
Arts administrator
Auditor
Bank manager
Building society manager
Bursar
Commercial account manager
Company secretary
Cost accountant
Currency trader
Financial controller
Insurance agent
Insurance adjuster
Lawyer
Market researcher
Post Office manager
Purser
Sales manager
Solicitor
Stock controller
Tax inspector

Concept formation
Account executive

Agricultural engineer
Aeronautical engineer
Aircraft engineer
Architect
Buyer
Computer systems analyst
Design engineer
Designer
Estimator
Fashion buyer
Fundraiser
Importer/exporter
Investment adviser
Landscape architect
Mathematician
Mathematics teacher
Merchandiser
Naval architect
Producer (films)
Stockbroker

Sequential logic
Accountant
Actuary
Aerodrome controller
Airline pilot

Astronaut
Chemical engineer
Computer technician
Database administrator
Deck officer
Electrical engineer
Electronics engineer
Food scientist
Health services administrator
Helicopter pilot
Horologist
Instrument and control engineer
Microelectronics engineer
Navigating officer
Coastal pilot
Programmer
Software engineer
Systems analyst
Technologist
Transport manager

Construct analysis
Account planner
Astronomer
Automobile designer
Building inspector
Building surveyor
Civil engineer
Economist
Ergonomist
Financial analyst
Geneticist
Geochemist
Geologist
Hydrographic surveyor
Information scientist
Manufacturing engineer
Mechanical engineer

Mining engineer
Surgeon
Nuclear physicist
Oceanographer
Physicist
Science teacher
Securities analyst
Statistician
Surveyor
Underwriter
Web designer
Web master

Power synthesis
Auctioneer
Broker
Business consultant
Chef
Chief executive
Civil servant
Cryptographer
Estate agent
Estate manager
Franchise operator
Head teacher
Hotel manager
Human resources manager
Managing director
Marketing manager
Manufacturing manager
Negotiator
Primary school teacher
Production manager
Property negotiator
Publisher
Purchasing manager
Sales executive

Level of score and IQ (intelligence quotient)

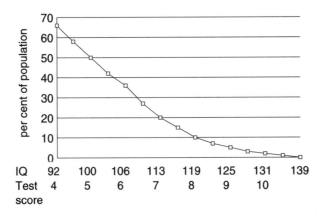

It must be remembered that the tests you have taken have not been controlled or developed in 'proper' test conditions and are therefore not expected to give you a true IQ score; they are intended only to illustrate the process and to get you as near as it is possible in a book to the 'real thing'. That said, you can use the graph above to see that a test score of 5 is equivalent to an IQ of 100, and that around 50 per cent of the population would be expected to obtain this score. A test score of 8, or IQ of 119, would be expected to be obtained by about 10 per cent of the population. People who obtain degrees or professional qualifications are mostly around the top 15 per cent of the population.

Thus, the higher your score on a test, the rarer is your aptitude and, therefore, the more 'saleable' or the greater demand there is likely to be for that type of potential. This may assist with guidance as to possible career direction.

It is, of course, also possible for you to rate your scores on the applied tests in the same way as the abstract tests using the graph above.

Numerical motivation test

In Part 4 you will establish your preferences in relation to different types of career that have an important numerical aspect.

Test 13: Numerical motivation test

This test looks at the direction you may wish to take in your career. The test intends to look specifically at types of career in which there is a numerical emphasis and where different types of numerical aptitude are likely to be required. In some the numerical content will be high, in others it will be slight, though still an essential part of that career.

You are given two activities and you have to decide upon the one you would prefer to do. Circle or tick your choice. Do not mark this book if it is not your own, but record your preferences on a separate sheet of paper by simply writing down the letter that corresponds with your choice.

Example

Would you rather:

a) Read the weather forecast on television   C

or

b) Collect samples for analysis from the sea bed   T

At this stage it does not matter whether you think yourself qualified to do the work, because the most important thing is to establish what type of work appeals to you most, not the actual work itself. How you might eventually move into a certain field of work is for later consideration.

Would you rather:

1. a) Design buildings   D

    or

    b) Measure distances between stars   R

2. a) Assess the breaking strain of metals   R

    or

    b) Calculate the probability of a possible future crisis B

3. a) Calculate profit margins on share transactions   B

    or

    b) Check the accuracy of business accounts   A

4. a) Record attendance and circumstances of
       hospital patients   A

    or

    b) Estimate costs of accident repairs   P

5. a) Plan and control flight paths of air traffic   P

    or

    b) Manage banking and loan facilities with customers   M

6. a) Cost and design automobile parts   D
        or
    b) Manage the finances of a college   B

7. a) Quantify the chemical constituents of genetic
        evidence   R
        or
    b) Ensure proper expenditure for an arts foundation   A

8. a) Advise on business mergers or selling a business   B
        or
    b) Inspect buildings for repair or building costs   P

9. a) Examine the financial transactions of a company   A
        or
    b) Persuade people to make donations for a certain
        cause   M

10. a) Design and cost the construction of a prototype
        racing yacht   D
        or
    b) Exchange currencies and deal with banking
        enquiries   A

11. a) Quantify data for a research project   R
        or
    b) Plot distances and expected arrival times for
        marine vessels   P

12. a) Negotiate costs and purchase component parts
        or materials   B
        or
    b) Calculate leave entitlements and bonus payments
        of staff   M

13. a) Decide upon sales potential and pricing of
         fashion goods   D
     or
     b) Calculate staff, machinery and other costs for
         running an estate   P

14. a) Establish a statistical survey of the incidence of
         a flu virus   R
     or
     b) Teach arithmetic to children   M

15. a) Estimate the expense of landscaping a large park   D
     or
     b) Organize a sports centre so that it operates
         profitably   M

16. a) Use computer modelling to find efficient solutions R
     or
     b) Gather data to judge the environmental impact of a
         new town   D

17. a) Project the costs and seek financial support to
         make a film   B
     or
     b) Use scientific instruments to calculate temperatures
         of the sea   R

18. a) Calculate tax arrears for companies or individuals A
     or
     b) Appraise a company's trading and recommend
         investment   B

19. a) Be in charge of financial matters on board a
       cruise ship   P
    or
    b) Maintain efficient records of items for sale in
       a business   A

20. a) Plan how to use staff, equipment and materials
       to create products   M
    or
    b) Keep records of the performance of machinery   P

21. a) Establish a sales target and how to obtain it   B
    or
    b) Establish the costs of preparing a celebratory
       banquet   D

22. a) Gather evidence of the falsifying of costs of
       goods in shops   A
    or
    b) Lecture in mathematics at university   R

23. a) Compose a cost efficient schedule for delivery
       of goods   P
    or
    b) Calculate the likely profit from publishing a
       series of books   B

24. a) Negotiate costs of holiday offers with hotels   M
    or
    b) Operate a postal office   A

25. a) Analyse and predict the performance of different
        companies   A
        or
    b) Create a web design within an agreed budget
        and time   D

26. a) Calculate the costs of building a bridge   P
        or
    b) Establish an efficient system for the retrieval of
        information   R

27. a) Estimate the value of property and seek potential
        purchasers   M
        or
    b) Calculate profit margins after shipping
        imported goods   B

28. a) Estimate the costs of sinking an oil well   P
        or
    b) Estimate the feasibility of producing a new type
        of vehicle   D

29. a) Advise upon insurance matters and calculate
        premiums   M
        or
    b) Undertake calibration checks of instrument
        reliability   R

30. a) Manage a hotel of 500 bedrooms and
        conference rooms   M
        or
    b) Create a building to a client's specification and
        budget   D

Marking the test

Count up your preferences by adding the number of times you have circled or ticked each letter that accompanies each statement. The maximum for each letter is 10. Record your scores below.

D	R	B	A	P	M
___	___	___	___	___	___

Motivation chart

Now place your scores in the motivation chart below. It is helpful to draw a line from the left-hand side of the chart up to your score. This will show in the clearest manner the strength of your preference for one broad field of work rather than another.

D – Creativity and design

| 0 | 1 | 2 | 3 | 4 | 5 | 6 | 7 | 8 | 9 | 10 |

R – Research and analysis

| 0 | 1 | 2 | 3 | 4 | 5 | 6 | 7 | 8 | 9 | 10 |

B – Business organization and sales

| 0 | 1 | 2 | 3 | 4 | 5 | 6 | 7 | 8 | 9 | 10 |

A – Finance and administration

| 0 | 1 | 2 | 3 | 4 | 5 | 6 | 7 | 8 | 9 | 10 |

P – Active and physical

| 0 | 1 | 2 | 3 | 4 | 5 | 6 | 7 | 8 | 9 | 10 |

M – People and management

| 0 | 1 | 2 | 3 | 4 | 5 | 6 | 7 | 8 | 9 | 10 |

Interpreting your results

Your highest scores indicate your strongest areas of preference. These suggest the broad type of work that appeals. Clearly, a low preference suggests a broad type of work that has less appeal. It is worth thinking carefully about your reasons for tending to reject this type of work. Of course, this does not mean that a specific job in this area may not appeal to you because there are so many facets to any career. However, to help you in thinking about the type of career that matches your preferences on the test, the following section provides a description of the type of work in each category.

In each of the following categories there is a list of careers. These are not exclusive; as has been said earlier, almost all jobs involve some amount of numerical aptitude. But it is not the intention of this book to include all possible careers – just a sample of those that are likely to depend to some degree on some kind and level of numerical aptitude to be carried out properly.

It is also the case that it is somewhat arbitrary to place a career in one category rather than another; some could go in two or three categories; some careers combine different types of work in different proportions, depending upon employer and nature of the specific job. For this reason, look at careers that appeal to you even if they are in an area of low preference from the test results, always asking yourself whether you have the type of inclination that would be satisfied by the tasks that career involves.

Career guidance

Creativity and design

These are careers in which there is a visual talent as well as a numerical one. This may be imaginative or abstract in an artistic or schematic way or may be exactly measured and defined as in the case of a plan or drawing. Numerical aptitude is required because of the precision required for calculating dimensions of surfaces and volumes as well as stresses, resistances, and so on. Most work is in a design office or studio.

Architect
Architectural technician
Automobile designer
Boat builder
Chef
Design engineer
Designer

Draughtsperson
Fashion buyer
Landscape architect
Naval architect
Planning technician
Town Planning officer
Web designer

Research and analysis

Careers in this area mainly have a scientific basis. They use research techniques of sampling and investigation that are applied to measurement and analysis of data or to samples of evidence. The numerical component may consist of advanced mathematics or straightforward counting and ordering of information. These careers are in government or related organizations as well as in private funded companies that depend upon scientific exploration or expertise.

Aeronautical engineer
Aeronautical technician
Agricultural engineer
Aircraft engineer
Astronaut
Astronomer
Chemical engineer
Computer technician
Cryptographer
Electronics engineer
Engineer
Food scientist
Geneticist
Geochemist
Geologist
Horologist

Information scientist
Instrument and control
  engineer
Laboratory technician
Market researcher
Mathematician
Microelectronics engineer
Oceanographer
Physicist
Programmer
Software engineer
Statistician
Surgeon
Systems analyst
Technologist
Web master

Business organization and sales

Careers in this area connect to business and the management of money, whether as profit, cost or investment. The numerical element relates to quantification of figures and attributing consequences to the way sums of money are spent or acquired. The environment is almost always commercial, in or dependent on the private sector.

Account executive
Actuary
Broker
Bursar
Business consultant
Buyer

Chief executive
Company secretary
Currency trader
Economist
Financial controller
Franchise operator

Importer/exporter
Investment adviser
Marketing manager
Merchandiser
Producer (films)
Publisher
Purchasing manager

Sales executive
Sales manager
Securities analyst
Space salesperson
Stockbroker
Turf accountant
Underwriter

Finance and administration

Careers in this area are connected with the efficient transfer, banking and safeguarding of money though allied records and information may also be dealt with. The numerical element is mainly with accounting and often complex means of consolidation, deduction and apportionment to do with statutory requirements. Careers are in private and public sectors as all organizations require proper governance.

Accountant
Account planner
Accounting technician
Administrator
Admissions clerk
Arts administrator
Auditor
Bank clerk
Building society assistant
Cashier
Civil servant
Clerk

Commercial account
    manager
Database administrator
Financial analyst
Health services administrator
Insurance adjuster
Post Office manager
Stock controller
Tax inspector
Theatre administrator
Trading Standards officer
Wages clerk

Active and physical

Careers in this area have some connections with the outside or 'out of the office' opportunity. This may involve inspection 'on site' or demand that key parts of the work take place outside, perhaps involving some discomfort or physical effort. The numerical element may involve estimation, measurement and other calculations related to machines, buildings or land. Numerical aptitude is used in a practical way in order to make something happen in the environment. There are careers in the private and public sectors.

Accident assessor
Aerodrome controller
Airline pilot
Building inspector
Building surveyor
Civil engineer
Coastal pilot
Cost accountant
Electrical engineer
Engineering officer
Ergonomist
Estimator

Estate manager
Farm manager
Helicopter pilot
Hydrographic surveyor
Manufacturing engineer
Mechanical engineer
Mining engineer
Navigating officer
Purser
Surveyor
Transport manager

People and management

Careers in this area are distinguished in some degree from others because of the focus they have on the care or attention they give to people. In other areas it is largely the information or process itself that is important, even though contact with people will also be part of any work. In this area numerical aptitude is essential but is secondary to the service to which it is applied so that 'people' skills of communication and leadership are essential.

Auctioneer
Bank manager
Building society manager
Deck officer
Fundraiser
Human resources manager
Estate agent
Head teacher
Hotel manager
Insurance agent
Lawyer
Legal executive
Licensee

Managing director
Manufacturing manager
Mathematics teacher
Negotiator
Primary school teacher
Production manager
Property negotiator
Science teacher
Solicitor
Sports centre manager
Teacher
Travel agent

Work style personality test

In Part 5 you will discover how your style of behaviour makes an impact on how you perform at work, how you relate best to the people you work with and will make you aware of possible areas of weakness.

Test 14: Work style personality test

The purpose of this test is to identify the typical ways you feel about people and situations as these will be important in any career you pursue. Answer in the way that reflects how you actually tend to be. Do not answer on the basis of how you wish you were.

You are given a statement and you must decide whether this is true of the way you behave or feel. The letters 'Y' and 'N' in the columns beside each statement mean 'Yes' this statement is true for you or 'No' it is not true for you. You must circle or tick either Y or N. You cannot score both and you cannot leave any statement out. If there is a statement where you cannot make up your mind, choose the answer that, on balance, tends to be more true.

The letters above the columns are not important at this stage. They will be used later to help you score the test. However, if this book is not your own, do not mark it, instead use separate sheets of paper to record your preferences by simply writing down the letter that corresponds with your choice and, later, use separate sheets to record analysis of your results.

The test is not timed. Begin when you are ready.

		O S	L C	A P	G I
1.	I'm the best person to decide how my work should be done				N Y
2.	I go out of my way to meet new people			Y N	
3.	I worry about making mistakes	N Y			
4.	I often make decisions without considering the consequences		Y N		
5.	It bothers me if I have a misunderstanding with someone	N Y			
6.	It is unusual for me to get angry		N Y		
7.	I usually speak my mind whatever people might think			Y N	
8.	I prefer it when someone else is in charge			N Y	
9.	I like to be with friends even if there's nothing to do				Y N
10.	Children should be protected rather than have to learn from their mistakes	N Y			
11.	I take whatever time and effort is required to get things right		N Y		
12.	I worry about troubles that might happen to people I know	N Y			
13.	I have a factual and logical mind	Y N			
14.	It takes a lot to upset me		Y N		
15.	I work best when I'm in a group				Y N
16.	I avoid annoying people			N Y	

17.	I like to do active things in my spare time		Y N			
18.	I can relate to how other people are feeling	N Y				
19.	I like noisy, busy places where people can have fun		Y N			
20.	I like doing risky, dangerous things		Y N			
21.	I rarely regret anything I've done	Y N				
22.	I do not think emotions should come into arguments	Y N				
23.	Friends can rely on me, even though they may be in the wrong					Y N
24.	I care about what people think of me				N Y	
25.	I do what is necessary even though some people may be offended				Y N	
26.	Worrying can sometimes keep me awake at night	N Y				
27.	I find it easy to turn to friends for help					Y N
28.	Having lots of friends is important to me					Y N
29.	I like to make up my own mind without interference from others					N Y
30.	I nearly always get my own way in an argument				Y N	
31.	I quickly get bored if I am unable to do something different		Y N			
32.	I like doing things spontaneously		Y N			
33.	I tend not to let other people take charge				Y N	
34.	I share lots of secrets with friends					Y N
35.	I'm reluctant to say what I think	N Y				
36.	I would rather listen than do the talking				N Y	
37.	I'm very competitive				Y N	
38.	I'm carefree and easy going		N Y			
39.	I avoid borrowing or lending personal things					N Y
40.	I talk to my friends about anything					Y N

Marking the test

Under each of the capital letters at the top of the columns count the number of responses you have. It does not matter whether these are Ys or Ns. Record your scores in the boxes below. The most you can have in any column is 10.

O	S	L	C	A	P	G	I
___	___	___	___	___	___	___	___

The scores are in pairs: O and S, L and C, A and P, G and I. In each pair, the letter with the higher score is the dominant letter. For example, if you had a score of 3 for the letter O and a score of 7 for the letter S then your dominant letter would be S. You also have to take one number from the other, in this case 7 minus 3, which is 4. Your final score is thus S4.

If you have a pair of letters where both scores are 5, then your final score is simply zero. Now take your four scores from the eight above and record them in the table below.

Dominant letter	___	___	___	___
Score	___	___	___	___

For each pair mark each score from the middle of the chart below. Thus, for the pair S and O, if your score is S4 your score is marked from the centre to the right of the chart on the 'O S' line.

On the chart below draw a line from the 0 at the centre to your score. If your score is 0 because both your scores in a pair were 5, mark the 0 on the line.

Work style personality chart

O																					S

Objective   Sensitive

10 9 8 7 6 5 4 3 2 1 0 1 2 3 4 5 6 7 8 9 10

C   L

Calm   Lively

10 9 8 7 6 5 4 3 2 1 0 1 2 3 4 5 6 7 8 9 10

P   A

Passive   Assertive

10 9 8 7 6 5 4 3 2 1 0 1 2 3 4 5 6 7 8 9 10

I   G

Independent   Group

10 9 8 7 6 5 4 3 2 1 0 1 2 3 4 5 6 7 8 9 10

Interpreting your results

From your chart you can see the four dimensions that most clearly define your personality. Most people have scores that show that although they tend to behave more one way than the other, they sometimes behave differently. It is when you have a clear disposition to one side of the chart that it becomes particularly important to ensure that this will fit in with your work as well as other activities in your life.

If your score was 0 on any pair then it shows that your behaviour is unlikely to be the extreme on either dimension, but that you might behave in both ways depending upon circumstances.

Objective or sensitive

In this context 'objective' means down to earth and realistic. It means you consider the facts of the matter, attempting to weigh evidence of what can be seen and measured, but that you discard possibilities and what might have been. Your preference will be to work with objects, facts or equipment where the end product is indisputably solid.

'Sensitive' here means that you accept emotions as part of a dispute, seeing these as important to be taken into consideration. In this case you will act upon feelings, finding it interesting to work with them rather than against them. Therefore you may be drawn towards work that has an artistic or creative side, or that involves understanding people's behaviour.

Calm or lively

Calm people can be relied upon to act deliberately. They see what is essential and act purposefully. They prefer to be slow and certain rather than hasty, because of a concern that they may miss something essential. Work that involves a methodical approach suits them well. If you are like this you will be effective in work that you can be certain of and where you feel in control by imposing order and regularity.

Lively people are spontaneous and enthusiastic. This can lead to haste in getting things done, but it does mean that new things are tried. If you are like this you will like to experiment. You may get quickly bored with routine as you like a challenging, fast-paced environment perhaps with an element of risk.

Passive or aggressive

'Passive' means that you tend to be of quiet character. You are likely to be accepting of what happens. You may not challenge adversity directly but avoid it or work around it rather than confront it directly. For this reason you are likely to be suited to more supportive or independent roles rather than ones that require forcefulness of character. People of this type often fit well into a team because they are accepting rather than demanding.

'Aggressive' types are inclined to be challenging. They often take the initiative about what should be done. For this reason they can be good leaders because they overcome possible self-doubt or embarrassment that may be the result of their assertiveness. This type of character frequently has the knack of getting things done with or through people.

Independent or group

'Independent' means inclined to work alone or in one's own way. If you are like this you prefer not to be interrupted or at least not for so long that you cannot press ahead with achieving what you want. You are self-reliant and do not require the support or approval of others when you make a decision.

If you scored high in the 'group' category, it means that you like to be involved with people. Having contact with others either as part of a team or with clients or customers is essential for you. You will want to include almost everybody you meet on a friendly, social basis. These outgoing tendencies are frequently associated with management and with other interfacing situations where social skills are important.

Understanding your personality style

Write on the line below the four words that describe your characteristics.

Style: _____

        (eg objective, calm, passive and independent)

Note that where you have a score of 0 on any pair you can describe yourself both ways, such as objective or sensitive, calm, passive and independent.

The four dimensions, when put together into a whole personality, produce 16 ways of behaving. If, on any dimension, you have middle scores, it is possible that you have different ways of behaving at different times so that, for example, rather than have one of the distinct 16 styles, you may have behaviour that sometimes corresponds with two or more of the styles.

First, identify your major style. From these, it is possible to make further suggestions as to the behaviour that will result. These considerations are important because they will affect your work and the people you work with. When you have identified the number that defines your style you can track that number in the charts that follow to gain some insight as to how you best fit in with an organization and its people.

The 16 styles

1. Objective Calm Passive Independent	2. Objective Calm Assertive Independent	3. Objective Lively Passive Independent	4. Objective Lively Assertive Independent
5. Objective Calm Passive Group	6. Objective Calm Assertive Group	7. Objective Lively Passive Group	8. Objective Lively Assertive Group
9. Sensitive Calm Passive	10. Sensitive Calm Assertive	11. Sensitive Lively Passive	12. Sensitive Lively Assertive
13. Sensitive Calm Passive Group	14. Sensitive Calm Assertive Group	15. Sensitive Lively Passive Group	16. Sensitive Lively Assertive Group

Your contribution to an organization

1.	2.	3.	4.
Logical analysis Discipline Reliability Change	Logical analysis Discipline Drive Change	Logical analysis Risk Reliability Change	Logical analysis Risk Drive Change
5.	**6.**	**7.**	**8.**
Logical analysis Discipline Reliability Continuity	Logical analysis Discipline Drive Continuity	Logical analysis Risk Reliability Continuity	Logical analysis Risk Drive Continuity
9.	**10.**	**11.**	**12.**
Intuition Discipline Reliability	Intuition Discipline Drive	Intuition Risk Reliability	Intuition Risk Drive
13.	**14.**	**15.**	**16.**
Intuition Discipline Reliability Continuity	Intuition Discipline Drive Continuity	Intuition Risk Reliability Continuity	Intuition Risk Assertive Continuity

Your contribution to the people you work with

1. Frankness Consistency Support Individuality	2. Frankness Consistency Direction Individuality	3. Frankness Excitement Support Individuality	4. Frankness Excitement Direction Individuality
5. Frankness Consistency Support Inclusion	6. Frankness Consistency Direction Inclusion	7. Frankness Excitement Support Inclusion	8. Frankness Excitement Direction Inclusion
9. Tolerance Consistency Support	10. Tolerance Consistency Direction	11. Tolerance Excitement Support	12. Tolerance Excitement Direction
13. Tolerance Consistency Reliability Inclusion	14. Tolerance Consistency Direction Inclusion	15. Tolerance Excitement Support Inclusion	16. Tolerance Excitement Direction Inclusion

Your possible weaknesses

1.	2.	3.	4.
Narrowness	Narrowness	Narrowness	Narrowness
Dullness	Dullness	Riskiness	Riskiness
Submissiveness	Invasiveness	Submissiveness	Invasiveness
Separateness	Separateness	Separateness	Separateness
5.	6.	7.	8.
Narrowness	Narrowness	Narrowness	Narrowness
Dullness	Dullness	Riskiness	Riskiness
Submissiveness	Invasiveness	Submissiveness	Invasiveness
Repetitiveness	Repetitiveness	Repetitiveness	Repetitiveness
9.	10.	11.	12.
Naivety	Naivety	Naivety	Naivety
Dullness	Dullness	Riskiness	Riskiness
Submissiveness	Invasiveness	Submissiveness	Invasiveness
Separateness	Separateness	Separateness	Separateness
13.	14.	15.	16.
Naivety	Naivety	Naivety	Naivety
Dullness	Dullness	Riskiness	Riskiness
Submissiveness	Invasiveness	Submissiveness	Invasiveness
Repetitiveness	Repetitiveness	Repetitiveness	Repetitiveness

The above indicate possible consequences of unvaried behaviour or behaviour at an extreme. For this reason, it is worth behaving in ways that are not within the repertoire of your normal type. This will enable you to test whether you are making the contribution you intend or responding to others in the way you intend.

Matching your personal style to a career

For this exercise and in completing the charts that follow, use your own paper if this is not your book. Write on the line below the four words that describe your style.

Style: _____

Now, referring to the Careers list on pages 169–173, write down the careers you would prefer.

1. _____

2. _____

3. _____

4. _____

5. _____

6. _____

etc.

The next step is to write down your preferred careers, your personality style and the aspects of your style that you have found in the charts above. Then think through how well each career seems to fit with the various aspects of your personality. Would there be any conflict? This does not mean that you should not consider the career as you may be wrong in what you assume about the career or the career may not give a conflict in certain organizations.

Similarly, do you think that you have any weaknesses in respect of a certain career that appeals to you? Again, do not reject it on this basis. Weaknesses are only weaknesses and may be overcome or turned into strengths. If so, how might any weakness be overcome? Again, your perception that you may have a weakness may be wrong.

This is a challenging and difficult exercise, particularly if you are uncertain about what the career may really demand or if you are unsure about whether your personality would be suitable. But it is one of the most worthwhile exercises to do because it increases your knowledge and awareness of both careers and your own potential.

Finally, it is always helpful to get some help and feedback from people who are experts such as career advisers or from people who know you such as family, friends and colleagues.

Career	My style	My contribution	My relationships	My possible weaknesses
	14. Sensitive Calm Assertive Group	14. Intuition Discipline Drive Continuity	14. Tolerance Consistency Direction Inclusion	14. Naivety Dullness Invasivenes Repetitiveness
Example: Accident assessor	Would it be too factual? Do I work in a group?	Would it be intuitive enough?	Would I get enough inclusion with people?	Would I be too forgiving and sensitive?

Now complete the table below with your own details and questions.

Career	My style	My contribution	My relationships	My possible weaknesses
1. _____				
2. _____				
3. _____				

Career	My style	My contribution	My relationships	My possible weaknesses
4. _____				
5. _____				
6. _____				

The process can be used with any career, including those in the Careers list below. As stated earlier, this list is not exhaustive, but has been compiled on the basis that each career will require numerical potential.

Careers list

Accident assessor
Accountant
Accounting technician
Account executive
Account planner
Actuary
Administrator
Admissions clerk
Aerodrome controller
Aeronautical engineer
Aeronautical technician
Agricultural engineer
Aircraft engineer
Airline pilot
Architect
Architectural technician
Arts administrator
Astronaut
Astronomer
Auctioneer
Auditor
Automobile designer
Bank clerk
Bank manager
Boat builder
Broker
Building inspector

Building society assistant
Building society manager
Building surveyor
Bursar
Business consultant
Buyer
Cashier
Chef
Chemical engineer (also Technologist)
Chief executive
Civil engineer
Civil servant
Clerk
Coastal pilot
Commercial account manager
Company secretary
Computer technician
Cost accountant
Cryptographer
Currency trader
Database administrator
Deck officer
Design engineer
Designer
Draughtsperson
Economist
Electrical engineer
Electronics engineer
Engineer
Engineering officer
Ergonomist
Estate agent
Estate manager
Estimator
Farm manager

Fashion buyer
Financial analyst
Financial controller
Food scientist
Franchise operator
Fundraiser
Geneticist
Geochemist
Geologist
Head teacher
Health services administrator
Helicopter pilot
Horologist
Hotel manager
Human resources manager
Hydrographic surveyor
Importer/exporter
Information scientist
Instrument and control engineer
Insurance agent
Insurance adjuster
Investment adviser
Laboratory technician
Landscape architect
Lawyer
Legal executive
Licensee
Loss adjuster (also Insurance adjuster)
Managing director
Marketing manager
Market researcher
Manufacturing engineer
Manufacturing manager
Mathematician
Mathematics teacher

Mechanical engineer
Merchandiser
Microelectronics engineer
Mining engineer
Naval architect
Navigating officer
Negotiator
Nuclear physicist
Oceanographer
Physicist
Planning technician
Post Office manager
Primary school teacher
Producer (films)
Production manager
Programmer
Property negotiator
Publisher
Purchasing manager
Purser
Sales executive
Sales manager
Science teacher
Securities analyst
Software engineer
Solicitor
Space salesperson
Sports centre manager
Statistician
Stock controller
Stockbroker
Surgeon
Surveyor
Systems analyst
Tax inspector

Teacher
Technologist
Theatre administrator
Transport manager
Town Planning officer
Trading Standards officer
Travel agent
Turf accountant
Underwriter
Wages clerk
Web designer
Web master

Further reading from Kogan Page

Other titles in the Testing series

How to Pass Graduate Psychometric Tests, 3rd edn, Mike Bryon, 2007

How to Pass the New Police Selection System, rev 2nd edn, Harry Tolley, Billy Hodge and Catherine Tolley, 2007

How to Pass Numeracy Tests, 3rd edn, Harry Tolley and Ken Thomas, 2006

How to Pass Numerical Reasoning Tests, rev edn, Heidi Smith, 2006

How to Pass Professional Level Psychometric Tests, 2nd edn, Sam Al-Jajjoka, 2004

How to Pass Selection Tests, 3rd edn, Mike Bryon and Sanjay Modha, 2005

How to Pass Technical Selection Tests, 2nd edn, Mike Bryon and Sanjay Modha, 2005

How to Pass the GMAT, Mike Bryon, 2007

How to Pass Professional Level Psychometric Tests, Sam Al-Jajjoka, 2004

How to Pass Verbal Reasoning Tests, 3rd edn, Harry Tolley and Ken Thomas, 2006

How to Succeed at an Assessment Centre, 2nd edn, Harry Tolley and Bob Wood, 2006

IQ and Personality Tests, Philip Carter, 2007

IQ and Psychometric Tests, 2nd edn, Philip Carter, 2007

IQ and Psychometric Test Workbook, Philip Carter, 2005

The Numeracy Test Workbook, Mike Bryon, 2006

Test Your IQ, Ken Russell and Philip Carter, 2006

Test Your Numerical Aptitude, Jim Barrett, 2007

Test Your Own Aptitude, 3rd edn, Jim Barrett and Geoff Williams, 2003

Interview and career guidance

The A–Z of Careers and Jobs, 14th edn, Susan Hodgson, 2007
Great Answers to Tough Interview Questions, 6th edn, Martin John Yate, 2005
Preparing the Perfect CV, 4th edn, Rebecca Corfield, 2006
Preparing the Perfect Job Application Form, 4th edn, Rebecca Corfield, 2007
Readymade CVs, 3rd edn, Lynn Williams, 2004
Readymade Job Search Letters, 3rd edn, Lynn Williams, 2004
Successful Interview Skills, 4th edn, Rebecca Corfield, 2006
The Ultimate CV Book, Martin Yate, 2002
The Ultimate Interview Book, Lynn Williams, 2005
IQ and Aptitude Tests, Philip Carter, 2007
The Ultimate IQ Test Book, Philip Carter and Ken Russell, 2007
The Ultimate Job Search Book, Lynn Williams, 2006
The Ultimate Job Search Letters Book, Lynn Williams, 2003
The Ultimate Psychometric Test Book, Mike Bryon, 2006